RAISE ^{IT!}

....

THE RELUCTANT
FUNDRAISER'S
GUIDE
TO RAISING MONEY

....

WITHOUT SELLING YOUR SOUL

CINDY WAGMAN

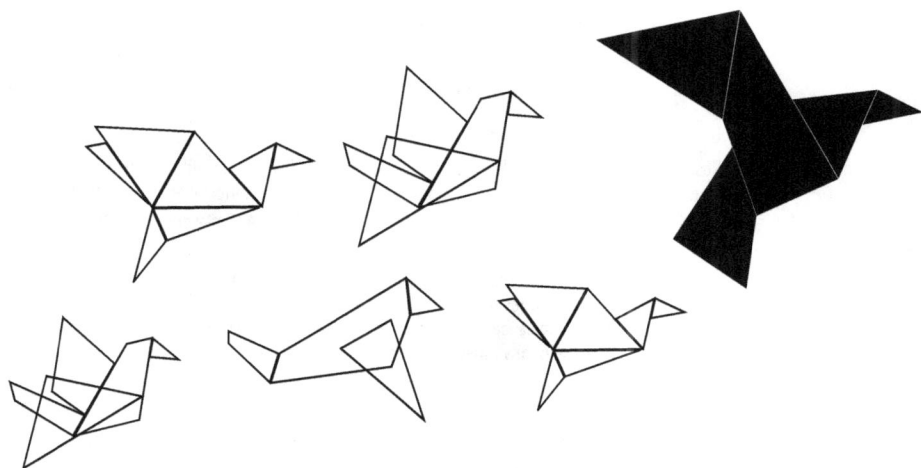

RAISE ^{IT!}

······································

THE RELUCTANT
FUNDRAISER'S
GUIDE
TO RAISING MONEY

······································

WITHOUT SELLING YOUR SOUL

Published in Canada, for Global Distribution

by YGTMedia Co. Publishing

www.ygtmedia.co/publishing

To order additional copies of this book:

publishing@ygtmedia.co

Publishing Editor: Tania Jane Moraes-Vaz

Editors: Kelly Lamb and Christine Stock

Book Designer: Doris Chung

Author photo by Nathalie Amlani

eBook Edition: Ellie Silpa

Paper Crane © Shutterstock/jarupan art

Bullhorn © Noun Project/Kusdarti

Cheque © Noun Project/DinosoftLab

Celebration © Noun Project/ibrandify

Goal © Noun Project/Saiful Muslim

Money © Noun Project/Designify.me

This book is dedicated to you! You're reading this because you are a change maker. You are dedicated to making the world a better place. You work with few resources but lots of heart. In my experience, this work is also undervalued and underappreciated—so, thank you.

TABLE OF CONTENTS

DOWNLOAD YOUR WORKBOOK!

Before you dig into this book, I highly recommend you download our FREE workbook that accompanies the book. If you purchased the book directly from our website, you should already have it.

If you borrowed the book or purchased it elsewhere, you can quickly and easily download the workbook from our website.

Keep up the good work!

Cindy

To download, go to: www.raiseitbook.com/bonus

INTRODUCTION

Welcome! Chances are you picked up this book because you want to change the world, create ripples of impact, and still be well-funded while pursuing your purpose. Whether you're an Executive Director (ED), board member, nonprofit staff, or volunteer, you've probably tried it all. All the fundraising strategies, the new ideas or hot trends, the coaching programs, the pricey consultants. If you were lucky enough to hire a fundraising staff member, it's likely that your organization has been hit with the high turnover plague that seems to be status quo in our sector. Whatever you've tried, it all leaves you feeling the same—not enough money; not the results you were hoping for; too many ideas, not enough action.

Everyone has *the* idea that might just be the rocket ship to launch your mission and raise funds, yet there's no one willing to go with you on your fundraising journey. You've probably lived it, too, which is why you're here with a copy of my book in your hands. Why? You guessed it. Fundraising feels hard, almost daunting. I hear it all the time: "How dare I ask someone to donate toward my cause and mission?"

But here's the kicker: How dare you *not* ask someone to donate toward your mission—a mission that could change lives.

When I first started The Good Partnership, I did a lot of research on what fundraising consulting entails. How consultants work. How they serve clients. This typically meant paying for coaching, developing a fundraising strategy, assessing team structure . . . all parts of traditional consulting. Everyone I spoke with had a similar perspective—all is sunny and bright on this side of the consulting relationship. Less work, more pay. Flexibility. Control. All the good things.

But no one prepared me for the horrible feeling I had when I sat across the table from my first coaching client week after week, sharing amazing advice, and having her report back that she had taken NO action.

This continued for about three or four weeks. We would meet in person at a cool, hip co-working space, where my team and I often worked. I would eagerly wait, excited to hear about her progress and any other updates. And each time we'd meet, the answer was always the same: "Nothing." No progress. No action. Instead, I heard lots of excuses. They were too busy. Something urgent came up. There wasn't enough time. Their donors don't want to be bothered.

To say that I was shocked would be an understatement. However, this was far more common than I realized, and it made me feel deflated, for many reasons. They were paying me a lot of money for my time, yet not implementing the strategies and recommendations I'd given them. And I felt so uncomfortable taking the organization's money knowing full well that it wasn't actually moving things forward for them.

I started losing sleep. All I wanted was for these organizations to be seen, to be experienced, to raise the funds their missions so rightfully deserved. They were doing incredible, life-changing work, and more people needed what they had to offer. I didn't want to be like the other consultants, taking money for advice while knowing that for small organizations, the advice would rarely lead to action.

So, I mustered up all my courage, I sat down with that coaching client, and I politely fired them.

You might be wondering, *who fires a client? If they're happy, who cares? It's their money.*

But I care! I didn't go into consulting to be able to work without account-ability, but that's what was happening. I started consulting to help small nonprofits. I love small nonprofits. This is the legacy I wanted to create in the world. Not by taking money knowing that none of the work would actually get done.

I took a step back and thought, *How can I make a real difference? How can I truly help small nonprofits in a way that will change their fundraising and grow their impact?*

And that's when it hit me: Our consulting model doesn't work the same way for smaller and medium-sized organizations.

And the deeper, underlying problem? So much of fundraising education is teaching people who WANT to fundraise the tactics to do so. Professional fundraisers who want to fine-tune their craft. But who was teaching the non-fundraisers who were shouldered with the responsibility of fundraising, when they would rather be doing anything but?

Imagine teaching an advanced law class to someone who doesn't want to be a lawyer! It just wouldn't work. Instead, those non-fundraisers end up overwhelmed and trying to copy what all the "thought leaders" in our sector preach. Instead of starting with the basics, they skip a few steps and end up overwhelmed and stuck.

This is not only the client I fired. I have seen this over and over again. I can't count all the times I'd receive a call from someone who would share with me their organization's fancy fundraising plan from three years ago, then tell me they didn't take action on the plan. I noticed a trend. Everyone was constantly caught up in trying what everyone else in the industry was doing.

"They hosted a gala and raised over $50,000, maybe we should do that."
"They hosted a pop-up event and raised over $150,000, we need to do that!"
"Perhaps we should encourage all our employees to fundraise. Grassroots efforts. Organically."
"We just need to get in front of Drake." (Yes, I have actually heard these exact words.)

That sounds great, dreamy even, but the reality is this: **None of it will work if you fundamentally do not want to fundraise.** It's forced action. And forcing yourself to do something that feels disconnected and unaligned at a visceral level will never yield the results you are looking for.

Best practices don't matter. Not if you haven't done the foundational work. Not if you have no interest in it. I always say, I'm never going to reach for the salad when it's sitting beside a pint of Ben & Jerry's. If you're uncomfortable with fundraising, there will always be something else you're going to reach for that feels more comfortable.

SO THEN WHAT DOES WORK?

You ready to hear it? I mean, we have a whole book together to journey through, but I will get right to it.

Through my research, decades of experience working with numerous nonprofit organizations, and their fundraising committees, boards, staff, etc., I have noticed a common theme: **Say hello to the "reluctant fundraiser."** Yes, I said it.

Why the reluctance, especially if it's for a good cause? I've asked myself that question far too many times to recall. Yet reluctance and hesitation are what I am met with whenever I connect with anyone and their fundraising goals. They can see it clearly—how their nonprofit can pave the way for social justice and change, but there's a stumbling block between their idealistic vision and the nitty-gritty implementation.

Every time I introduce myself as a fundraiser, I am met with the exact same response:

"Wow! That must be a really hard job. I could never do that."

"It takes a certain kind of person to work in the nonprofit sector."

Or the worst: "I have no money—sorry." (As IF I walk around asking random people for money all the time. Ha!)

What if we pause for a moment and think about what's the underlying factor behind the hesitation to fundraise? What if we identify *why* fundraising makes you feel icky—the stories that are running rampant in your mind—and why you think you cannot be successful at fundraising?

Ultimately, our organizations are only as successful as the resources we can bring to them. And yes, this includes philanthropy.

Our mission, our desire to have ripples of impact throughout the world, to do good, and pave change in society requires us to step up and lead. Step up and raise money.

I realize that this is often where the hesitation starts to seep in, that lump in your throat, your sweaty palms. Or perhaps you feel like you're going against the whole principle of "being charitable." Maybe it feels like you're selling your soul, so to speak. Even just thinking about fundraising ignites a series of physical and emotional reactions for people. Whatever the case may be, fundraising doesn't have to feel this way!

I'll say that again: Fundraising doesn't have to take place in its traditional discourse. It *can* and *should* excite you, fuel you into your purpose, and bring tons of funds back to your organization so you can create the impact you desire. And that in a nutshell is the purpose of this book.

My intention with this book isn't for this to be yet another book about ideas and tactics. No, thank you. We have enough of those. There are no quick fixes in this book. Or easy ways to raise your next $100 or your next $100,000.

Rather, what you will find is:

- A deep dive into addressing the root causes behind your inaction, or the reluctance that precedes it.
- An opportunity to unlock and evolve your mindset around fundraising by activating you to take action toward your fundraising goals consistently. Be it inviting ten people to your online event, reaching out to five companies for sponsorships, writing social media content, or all of the above, especially if you are a small organization that is trying to grow.
- The ability to identify the underlying issues that plague smaller organizations—even larger ones; reluctant fundraisers exist everywhere—because nobody has shared a way that feels good for them to show up, share their mission, and take up space.
- The ability to identify scarcity and self-sabotage, and to navigate all the mind drama that takes over your effort and impact.
- Tools and integration methods to help you tap into your confidence, master your ability to spark excitement about your nonprofit, and ignite others to be inspired to give.

- Advice that works for EVERY type of donor—individuals, corporations, foundations, and more.
- Next steps and useful resources to spur you on once you've finished the book.

Fundraising and the way we go about it is changing. Traditional philanthropy in Western society, especially as we see it in the news, on TV shows, and in the movies typically looks like incredibly rich folks donating heaps of money to organizations, usually the big ones. And in my opinion, that is a very broken model perpetuating unhealthy power dynamics.

This type of story about philanthropy is just one of the narratives we need to rewrite to really unleash the power of philanthropy and to unlock the fundraising capacity of reluctant fundraisers.

When we stereotype or typecast *who* can or cannot donate, we limit ourselves, we limit our organizations, we limit the amount of money we can receive, and most of all, we limit these incredible people from donating whatever it is they desire to donate to a good cause. All because they didn't fit the traditional view or model of philanthropy.

Hot tip: It is not up to us to decide who can or cannot give. When we do that, we take away their fundamental right to decide if and how to invest in the world that they want to create to move in.

Instead, I want you to start employing a new mindset, a new belief. Think of fundraising as creating a movement in support of the cause. Mobilizing people, foundations, and companies who care. The donors are perpetually rigged in your favor when they a) see YOU believe in your cause and its mission and the impact it can create; and b) when that same excitement ripples onto them, making them lifelong, devoted fans who will always come through with funds, no matter what.

I want you to start thinking of *how* you can cultivate, build, and rally support that then affects the change you're wanting to create and what the organization you are working with needs. I want you to dream of all the possibilities and then act on them. Give no room to the limitations that will crop up. Believe me, I've heard them all. Scarcity mindset doesn't only pertain to money. It pertains to how we go about everything—what we think we can or cannot do. We are so hardwired to look at what we can't do instead of what is possible. How can we move the needle forward even one degree? And we then project these same limitations onto our potential donors. Instead, look at the big picture and recommit to the impact you desire to create.

It's easy to throw money at problems rather than tackle them yourself, am I right? I've seen small organizations spend almost $20,000 on hiring an expert to create a fundraising plan that never gets implemented and collects dust for the next three or four years. In smaller organizations, fundraising feels like a challenge because the CEO is often the one fundraising, on top of their already full workload. Reluctant fundraisers are so quick to pass the buck. They'd rather recruit that one board member who has experience fundraising or corporate connections and hope they'll do it all. When I ask organizations what they would do if I wrote them a check for $100,000, the number one answer is to hire a fundraiser. Not just because they want to grow their fundraising capacity, but because they want someone else to shoulder that responsibility so they don't have to.

Around the board table, it might look like lots of fundraising ideas with little follow-through. Or worrying about branding and communications as a precursor to fundraising (guess what—it's not!). They might decide to invest in a "good pitch deck" because that will surely solve all their fundraising problems (can you sense my sarcasm?).

Offloading the problem altogether results in disengagement from the cause and mission. Anyone who you are trying to engage in giving can sense the disconnection in energy, passion, and presence, which then leads to a vicious cycle of no funds raised because we aren't addressing the elephant in the room: *Why does it feel uncomfortable to fundraise?*

Other times, as I shared in my example earlier, someone pays me a lot of money to coach them, but they never take action because they haven't addressed the underlying issue. They fundamentally don't want to fundraise.

And sometimes, it's a case of the "evergreen ideas graveyard" where every idea is resurrected over and over again, yet nobody wants to step up, lead, and take action. I hear the excuses—I'm too busy; we need this in place first; I need more help and support.

Bottom line—they are uncomfortable with fundraising at its core and hence feel comfortable forever exploring ideas without really executing them.

Whatever the reason, I am here to help you navigate this, address the root cause, and get back to your mission with renewed passion. I want to empower you with the tools, strategies, and most of all with the mindset that there are always people who desire to invest in your organization for exactly what it is you have to offer. People who want to support your mission with their dollars.

Throughout this book, we are going to examine what prevents you from showing up and doing the work. We will rewire certain thought patterns and behaviors and break down limiting beliefs. We will unlock and help you master your mindset so you can stop letting self-sabotage run the show. We will address your language—your self-talk, which then translates to self-fulfilling prophecies—positive or negative. We will quit wasting money on trying to offload and numb out your problems and actually do the inner work that is needed so that you can become a master at fundraising. In fact, you will learn how to make fundraising *your* art, because your mission requires it. It requires you to be authentic, raw, and 100 percent you, which means saying bye-bye to traditional scripts and tactics. Here, we master the mindset (the way you think about something) and the heart-set (the way you feel about something), and bring back the confidence and passion along with some strategy.

People want to give to your cause. They want to see you succeed and change the world. Your mission is too important to let it sit there and collect more dust before you can ever raise the funds it needs to go make a difference. Well, let's change that with this book and help you *raise it!*

WHAT GOT YOU HERE WON'T GET YOU THERE (OUR SECTOR IS BROKEN)

I'll cut right to the chase.

Our sector is broken.

Over 80 percent of charities are considered "small," but how we talk about and teach fundraising is tailored to large organizations. With conventional structures of philanthropy, small organizations are often left scrambling, frustrated, and burned out.

When most people think of fundraising, they think of lavish galas and auctions. Or multimillion-dollar donations from well-known philanthropists to name a new hospital wing or building. Or the big run where all of your friends are emailing you links so you can donate to their campaign. Occasionally, it's the adorable and precocious child who raises $1,000 for the local hospital (so heartwarming). These are the fundraising headlines that make the news and attract our attention. And yes, they are fundraising. But they're only a small fraction of it.

You mean there are other ways to fundraise and not feel sleazy doing it?
Yes. Yes, there are.

Here's what I often see happening within our industry, which usually boils down to these four root causes. I'm here to help you determine which one of these continues to hinder the success your mission could have. Are you ready?

1. We focus on big organizations, but it's the smaller ones that often need our help the most.
2. We typecast donors as "haves" and "have-nots."
3. We operate from a lack and scarcity mindset.
4. We love ideas, but we don't take action.

See, that wasn't too bad!

I want you to take a second, pause your reading, and think about which of these root causes sounds familiar to you—and don't worry if they all do; I'm not here to judge.

The good news is that you're going to start to build a different relationship with fundraising (and with yourself) as you do the strategic, energetic, and emotional work associated with fundraising.

Before we dig into the meaningful shifts that are going to happen for you, I want to take a few minutes to introduce you to the underlying concept of this book—leveraging neuroscience. Don't be alarmed. I'm not going to get too technical, instead I'm going to focus on some principles around how our brain works and how that governs our behaviors. It's not scary, but it is important. You see, reluctant fundraisers are dealing with fundamentally different barriers (learned behaviors) than "chosen fundraisers." They view fundraising as something negative, a necessary evil that they need to do even though they'd rather do anything else. And because they view fundraising with such distaste, it's no wonder they don't enjoy it or feel they are good at it. And why they often avoid doing it. As you'll see in the coming chapters, we are going to start by understanding how our brains have reinforced some of the pervasive myths and problems with fundraising for smaller nonprofits, and in Section 2, I'm going to show you how to rewire your brain for fundraising success.

You are here because you're an action taker who is ready to change the way your organization does fundraising. And you know that what got you to where you currently are won't get you to where you want to be.

Where do you want to be? Sometimes, we have a hard time imagining a different way of fundraising. It's not your fault. You see, we've been told the same stories about fundraising over and over again so they become the truth to us. We start to believe that these are the only ways to do it.

So, what does an alternative look like? Who do you want to be as a fundraiser?

You want to be the person who is successfully raising more money for your organization. And notice, I didn't just say you want to raise more money because that's not it. **You really want to be that person.** You want to feel successful. You want to be confident. You want to own it!

When we talk about being a good fundraiser, it means you are in control. Let me repeat that. You are in control! That's right. Oftentimes, we think of fundraising as being at the mercy of others. Will or won't this person give? Is our brand strong enough? Is our board connected enough? The answer is (and this might be hard to hear) IT DOESN'T MATTER! That's right. **You're the driver of this journey.**

Brendon Burchard, an author and coach who studies the habits of high performers, wrote, "When you knock on the door of opportunity, do not be surprised that it is work who will answer." Right?

We know we have to do the work. That's why we're here. But I'm here to show you what work you need to be doing to be the most effective, so you can create the impact you envision and change lives with your mission.

CHAPTER 1

CHANGE STARTS WITH A SIMPLE DECISION

Did you know that approximately 90–95 percent of the decisions we make are unconscious? I'm not just talking about which outfit to put on in the morning or what to eat for breakfast. Those are often decisions we know we are making. It's estimated that we make 35,000 remotely conscious decisions each day. On top of that, there are all the unconscious decisions like which way to turn our head, when to stop eating, how to hold a pen, etc. Ever heard of decision fatigue? This is why we experience it!

We make these decisions without a second thought—almost on auto-pilot—because our brain is designed to make those easily. Our awareness isn't as heightened when making certain decisions, especially if they are a part of our regular daily habits. Think of your morning routine. Even if you wake up alert and ready to take on the day, there are probably some decisions that take place much like a light switch. For instance, you brush your teeth, wash your face, get a workout in, hydrate, and brew a cup of coffee while you slip in for a quick shower before you get dressed and then log onto your laptop for work. In reality, there are eight very distinct steps that have been completed here; however, your brain has managed to make this a fluid habit because you do it so often. The only time your awareness would be heightened is if you totally skipped one of the usual steps in this routine.

Hot tip: Our brain simplifies complex decisions into short-cuts or neural pathways. This allows those decisions to be made faster and with less effort, preserving your brain's energy for more important things. Brilliant, right?

I think of these neural pathways like driving routes.

Think back to a time when you were starting a new job. It's your first time driving to your new workplace. And of course, you're checking your GPS, and you're alert and attentive to all the landmarks you see en route. You are aware of all your surroundings. That right there is your brain creating a new (albeit lite) neural pathway as a result of all the micro decisions along the way.

And now a month or two has passed since you started your new job, and the drive to work feels easy, effortless, like you could do it in your sleep. You're in autopilot mode. You don't need to pay attention to all the landmarks and exit signs. You end up at the office and it seems like no big deal.

Now you aren't expending a lot of mental energy or capacity to remember every detail. This means that your neural pathway is well defined as a shortcut.

Imagine if a whole month later, you are driving to a meeting at a building that's located close to your office. You get in the car and are on your way. However, when you've parked your car and you look around, you realize that you're at your office instead of the correct office for the meeting that's a few blocks down. *This* is exactly what functioning on autopilot looks like. And this occurs all the time. Our brain will always choose the shortcut, the easy way out even when we know we have to do something slightly different. Our brains default to the quick and easy ways because it's evolutionary. It feels good, safe, comfortable, and familiar.

This is how our brain governs our life.

When I used to train at my local gym, I remember my trainer telling me, "Change starts with a simple decision, but then it takes approximately three weeks for you to feel the changes internally, five weeks for you to notice a slight difference, and about ten weeks for anyone else to notice any visible changes."

In fact, according to neuroscientist Dr. Shannon Irvine, if you are working on a new habit or behavior, it takes about 21 days for your new neural pathway to start meaningfully competing with the old behavior or neural pathway. At about 70 days, the new one becomes dominant.

So, to overcome our barriers around fundraising, we need to rewire our brains. Are you ready to discover how successful fundraisers think? Let's do it!

As you can probably tell from the example, these neural pathways and shortcuts are created and deepened through repetition. I will never forget the experience of trying to teach my kids how to read. Reminding them of the pronunciation of the same word over and over again. We don't think about reading as breaking down sounds and syllables, but that's what our brain is doing. We've just developed the shortcuts to make it easy and fast. Same thing with walking! How many steps does it take for walking to become second nature? I haven't counted, but my sore back from hunching over toddlers can attest that it's a LOT.

But it's not just repetition that influences the neural pathways we create. There are patterns that are designed and developed to protect us from harm.

I want you to pause again and think about this—what does harm look like when it comes to fundraising? Is it the anguish of being rejected? The risk of hurting a friendship? Just the discomfort of trying something new?

One pattern that shows up consistently in our neural networks is that our brain overemphasizes negative things and underemphasizes the positive. We have a human tendency to fixate on the negative. And what you focus on is what gets amplified. Perhaps you send an email to your email list and one person responds saying, "You email me too much." However, as a result of you sending that one email, 100 people donate. That's a massive positive! But your mind will tend to focus on that one negative comment, which will far outweigh the success you had. You start doubting yourself. *Should I ask less often? Am I sending too many emails? Yikes, people are going to start unsubscribing.* You might have just raised $1,000, but that one negative response gets amplified in your brain. Sound familiar?

These patterns hinder us and our fundraising success. We are programmed to survive. Thriving feels new to us. We are used to always looking for anything that can go wrong instead of focusing on the positive. And here's a common truth: whatever we choose to fixate on, expands. Our energy goes where our focus flows.

Or has this happened to you? Perhaps you want to buy yourself a white Tesla (that's my kids' current fixation, but pick your favorite brand), and the moment you've made up your mind about it, you start seeing shiny white Teslas everywhere you go. As a result, you take that as a sign that you should go ahead and purchase that car. Truth is, there are a lot of white cars on the road, but because your mind has fixated on a white Tesla, that is exactly what it will go out of its way to find, while ignoring all the other car brands that also come in white. This is called the **Baader-Meinhof Phenomenon**. It's a frequency illusion when your awareness of something increases because your brain is now fixated on something, meaning it seems more frequent. In reality, there are no more white Teslas on the road than before you thought about getting one.

This can very easily create an "everyone else is doing it this way" fallacy. For example, let's say someone suggests that your organization needs to host a gala to raise money. Now, your brain is going to pay more attention every time it notices an organization like yours hosting a gala. All of a sudden, to your mind, it's like EVERYONE is hosting galas and that's one of the best ways to fundraise (which it's not—at least, not usually). So, while you might have been hesitant to host a gala before, now it seems inevitable because of the Badder-Meinhof Phenomenon.

Another familiar pattern is **Confirmation Bias**, which is how our brains ascribe meaning to things based on our existing beliefs. For example, let's say you text someone to make plans, but you don't get a response from the text. If you already believe that the person you texted is someone who wants to see you, you interpret the lack of response as meaning that they're just busy. However, if you already believe that the person may not like you, then you interpret the lack of response as evidence to support the fact that they don't like you.

To bring it closer to home, I've seen Confirmation Bias really affect people's self-beliefs around their fundraising abilities. Most people will say something like, "I'm not a good fundraiser," which is a way of declaring an identity (of not being a fundraiser). So, if your existing belief is that you're not a fundraiser, your brain will search for evidence to support this belief and will ignore any evidence that contradicts it. I've done fundraising audits for organizations that insist their fundraising is terrible, but when I look at the numbers, it's absolutely not true. From the outside, I can clearly see their success, but because the individual has primed their brain to support that belief, it distorts the data so all they see is failure and proof of their point that they're bad at raising funds.

And last but not least, we have the **Status Quo Bias**, which typically occurs when our brains would prefer that things stay the same. We are wired to stay safe, which means taking little to no risks, avoiding discomfort, and resisting learning something new. A couple of everyday examples can be found in what we wear and what we eat. Did you know that most of us only wear 20 percent of our wardrobe most of the time? Even though we were the ones who bought our clothes, we still gravitate to the same reliable options over and over because it's easy, it's safe. How often have you gone grocery shopping and bought the same items, week after week, instead of buying some new spices or ingredients and changing up your predictable menu?

With Status Quo Bias, there is little to no growth because there isn't a deep desire for change; it is safer to do what has always been done or stick with a decision that was made previously. **This happens EVEN when the cost to change is small and the importance and benefit of that change is high.** I mean, do I even need to identify work examples of this one? How about choosing to continue to host a fundraising event that doesn't net any money (and don't say you're holding out hope for it to be more lucrative in the future) in lieu of taking all the time and energy you put into hosting the event and instead redirecting it toward a more productive fundraising strategy. Or having a full-time admin position who spends 90 percent of their time on tasks that can be easily automated because you don't like investing in technology or changing your systems and processes. Even if the technology option is WAY cheaper, you still see it as an added cost. And even if you could take that 90 percent of the person's time and have them work on programming or fundraising or anything that contributes more directly to your mission, you still resist. There is a lot that hinders our fundraising success before we ever engage with potential donors. However, the sooner we begin to identify these patterns, the sooner we can start rewiring them and write a new story.

Just as there are patterns to how our brains are wired, there are common patterns and beliefs that I see with how we show up for fundraising as reluctant fundraisers. The rest of this section will dive into those, then in the next section we'll start to explore how to rewire these shortcuts and start raising money!

$ DOLLAR FOR YOUR THOUGHTS

Grab a notebook or your free workbook you downloaded and pen and get comfortable. We are going to identify some biases that you may hold that hinder your success as a fundraiser. Awareness always precedes clarity and change. So let's get to it.

1. What are some biases and beliefs you hold about fundraising? How do you really feel about it?
2. Which one of these biases do you encounter frequently?
3. What is the outcome of these biases? How have they shown up for you at work or in your fundraising?

CHAPTER 2

UNPOPULAR OPINION—SIZE DOES NOT MATTER

It's true! You can fundraise no matter the size of your organization.

You do not need to be one of the big sharks in the ocean to create an impact or make yourself known. In fact, you can be your own blend of unique, small or solo but mighty in the ocean of fundraising. You don't need to outsource your fundraising. Yes, I, Cindy Wagman of The Good Partnership (in case you didn't already know, my business does outsourced fundraising), am telling you this. And for good reason!

I started fundraising consulting after almost fifteen years as an in-house fundraiser in organizations both large and small. I knew I wanted to work with small charities and felt that I could meaningfully help them raise more money for their important work.

I started to learn about the consulting business and quite frankly, what I learned shocked me. So many nonprofits had amazing ideas but no clear path to bringing those visions to light. They felt so uncomfortable tackling the financial side of things that they just didn't. Or their reluctance to manage the money side of things, which often meant the fundraising side, meant that many of them were barely hanging on and were rarely growing.

All too often they thought that hiring a consultant to tell them how to raise the necessary money to stay afloat would solve all their problems. So, many small organizations would squirrel away enough money to pay large amounts to amazing consultants (and yes, they are good at what they do) to develop a three- to five-year fundraising strategy that had absolutely no practical value to them. I'd start working with a client and they'd proudly show me the thorough fundraising strategy that was developed years earlier.

What had been done to advance that strategy since then?

NOTHING. UGH!

This was not a one-time occurrence.

No, I have seen this time and time again, in countless organizations. And it doesn't make any sense.

I'm not saying you shouldn't hire consultants who are incredible at what they do and who will help you move the needle toward the goals you have for your mission. But having a plan that you don't implement isn't that different than having no plan. And paying for a plan that you're going to ignore is like wasting all that money. You cannot outsource any work before you square away your feelings and beliefs about fundraising. There is a BIG difference between outsourcing some of the work because you are growing and need more support versus outsourcing the work because you just don't want to deal with it. And this is what I've seen for small nonprofits over and over again. You don't want to fundraise. Fundraising feels like begging. It's too difficult and uncomfortable for you. So, you decide to just get someone else to do it.

What's even stranger is that we think that "best practice generators" that typically work for larger organizations will work for smaller organizations. That's right, you can't just copy the Ice Bucket Challenge or the million-dollar gala or massive celebrity endorsement. Small organizations spend so much time spinning their wheels trying to copy what they see that they neglect to do the real, consistent, meaningful, community-building fundraising work that has to happen to build sustainability and impact.

I often see small organizations almost take a backseat energetically and feel disconnected from their vision and their mission because they're operating on strategies that aren't customized to what they need. This one-size-fits-all approach needs to stop.

I ask myself every single time, *How are we, as consultants, okay with this?*

I, for one, am not. I decided to change it. Which is why, together with my team at The Good Partnership, we focus on fundraising mindset, implementation, and consistency.

Small organizations (especially ones without fundraising staff, which is who we typically work with) are not positioned to implement fundraising strategies because they are too broad, too vague, and have no specific deliverables. Yes, we all want to build a culture of philanthropy. We all want to build diverse revenue. You don't need to pay a consultant tens of thousands of dollars to tell you that.

This is linked to the fact that we love ideas, but we don't take action. We are constantly trying to find external solutions for internal problems.

How about building a fundraising plan instead? A plan that works for you, for your unique mission. A plan where deliverables and milestones are mapped and feed into your big vision and annual goals. This way, whether your fundraising is done by fundraising staff, the ED, the board or volunteers, a plan keeps everyone on the same page and defines success with a map on how to achieve it and grow your mission. A plan is a road map. It's the bridge between how to take those ideas and turn them into action. A plan might be for 90 days, six months, or one year, but not longer. Most of all, a good fundraising plan is aligned and authentic for your organization, and it's built on a mindset of abundance and of embracing fundraising.

There is a huge emphasis on growth for all nonprofits, but especially small ones. It's almost an obsession. How do we grow more? How do we raise more money? What happens if we don't grow enough this year?

Which then begs me to ask the question: What happens when a small nonprofit doesn't grow? Is there a shelf-life for small organizations?

Your mission is far too special and very much needed in the world for you to sit back and let it collect dust because you're trying to do all the things, be all the things, and approach it with a one-size-fits-all mindset.

Your mission and impact are the biggest driving factors behind your decisions around growth and fundraising.

Small organizations are often nimble, community focused, and the leaders of change. Think of your favorite local nonprofits that you love supporting. Chances are the reason you love supporting them is because they are so connected to the heartbeat of their mission: their WHY.

Your decisions around growth should start with a strong rationale that drives back to your impact.

Sure, bigger organizations might have the clout behind them such as longevity, a dedicated fundraising department, corporate galas, and more. But you have heart. You have grit. You have passion. You have your strong WHY. Which is why size does not matter as long as you continue to stay connected to your vision and create a plan to help you bring it to life.

And that WHY is also how you are going to find donors who are excited and enthusiastic about giving. These are not unicorns I'm describing—such donors exist in abundance when you do the work right.

Before we wrap up this chapter, I want to share another story with you.

I met a woman online who, when I introduced myself, said, "I run a small grassroots nonprofit that I'm pretty much supporting all by myself with little financial help from others. I know I really have to get over asking for money, but it's hard." After a little back and forth, she updated me with the following: "I walked out my door today and had a conversation with my neighbor about my nonprofit, and she was eager to assist, as well as offered to fundraise for the cause."

Donors who care about your work exist all around. Sure, they might not be the same donors who attend the $1,000-a-plate galas, but sometimes they are the same. When we start to embrace the fact that people **want** to give and they care about your mission and work, then we start to see a new community of donors who can both fund our work and be part of the awesome communities we are building. Let's stop trying to chase the big organizations, the pricey consultants, and offloading of the work, and embrace the power of fundraising as a tool to not just fund, but to enhance and serve your mission.

$ DOLLAR FOR YOUR THOUGHTS

Let's bring it back to the basics. Get your pen and workbook ready. We are going to get aspirational with your vision.

1. Why is this cause close to your heart?
2. How will this help your community?
3. Take out a voice recorder (most phones have them) and I want you to talk to me and tell me why you are passionate about your organization. Then, listen back to it and even write it down. Is this different to your mission and vision? If so, your mission and vision might need to be updated.
4. Recommit to that passion.
5. Take a picture of it with your phone and make this your screensaver on your phone or your computer. Write it on sticky notes and put them all over the place.
6. Practice what you preach. Almost everyone I know gives to charity, whether it's $10 or $10,000. Think for a moment about your contributions and make a decision to support the organizations you think are doing the important work. Bonus points if those organizations are small and mighty!

CHAPTER 3

THE BATTLE OF THE HAVES VERSUS THE HAVE-NOTS

It really doesn't have to be a battle. I promise. But frequently, we typecast people into two groups: those we think can give to our mission and those we think cannot. Of course, this is another shortcut our brains are making. When we are so primed to think of donors as those who are "wealthy," we also believe that those who are not "wealthy" don't give.

So, here is what happens:

Much of fundraising has been focused on "finding people with money" or focusing solely on corporations and bigger foundations. We tend to focus only on those who appear to have it all—rich and powerful CEOs with designer wardrobes, luxury cars, living in exclusive penthouses or in expensive private school neighborhoods. We assume "giving" can only take place within those circumstances, with those people. However, *who* gives or donates to our mission is not limited to the "wealthy."

It's certainly not our fault that we think this way. Going back to "news-worthy" fundraising I mentioned in the previous chapter, these are the archetypes of philanthropy perpetuated in our society. These are the stories we hear over and over so that they become mental shortcuts. But dig a little deeper or look toward other cultures and there are deep, beautiful, and old histories of community-based giving that recognize the role each of us play in philanthropy.

I mentioned earlier in my introduction that when we typecast who we think can donate versus who won't want to donate, we limit our missions from receiving help from all directions. It isn't up to us to decide this for people. By making assumptions of *who* can or cannot donate to our mission, we take away the power to invest in the change we want to see in the world.

Everyone can give. Giving isn't limited to the wealthy.

We live in a society where petitions and funds are raised at the drop of an online link. All that you need is an unapologetic and passionate rally around *why* someone should contribute even a dollar toward your mission. I bet you're thinking about it right now. Think about all the times you've seen a campaign—be it to help someone raise funds for a family battling a hardship or for someone to go chase their dreams. If you take a look at the donor list, donations range from $1 all the way to a couple thousand. So, why is it that you continue to assume that it is only the "rich" who can donate?

Are you ready for this? Giving isn't about money.

Let me say that again. Giving is not about money. It's not about the size of a check. Giving is an act of love. An act of defiance. An act of caring. An act of protest. It can be any and all of these things. And it's not up to you in your fundraising to decide who can love, defy, care, or protest.

Giving is changing, whether we are on board with it or not. Younger generations give to causes they deeply care about. Giving is now accessible in one click. Much like shopping online during a lockdown, donating to a good cause has become incredibly accessible, and raising funds online often takes little to no time. And guess what? Many times these causes aren't "registered." People aren't giving for the tax receipt or as a tax-reducing tool, they are giving because they care. Because they see it as an act of activism. Or of "putting your money where your mouth is."

The pandemic changed the fundraising landscape significantly and reduced the gap between who *we* presume can or cannot donate. It leveled the playing field. Everyone could donate—their time or a few dollars—to share the mission.

According to the latest trends as per *The Giving Report* published by CanadaHelps.org and Imagine Canada:

- **Young donors are giving to causes they deeply care about.** Young donors who don't necessarily have a very high income have stepped up in major ways during the pandemic. Not only are they giving to individual charities, they are also donating to cause-based funds that will benefit a larger number of charities.

- **Because of the diversification of donors, important issues and sectors are being supported in more significant ways.** For instance, we're seeing an increase for individual donations to Indigenous charities, and to the arts and cultural sector. And we are seeing an increase in donations related to education, families, and children.

I had this conversation recently on our podcast with Nneka Allen, Camila Vital Nunes Pereira, and Nicole Salmon where we were talking about the traditions of philanthropy in their communities. Philanthropy for them has been about collective responsibility. As a Jewish person, I was taught the same things. Ten percent of whatever you make (regardless of how much that is) is set aside for the community. Somewhere along the way, these stories around philanthropy started to get lost in the professionalization of the sector and the dominance of large organizations and larger donations.

While I want to say that giving is changing, the reality might be that we are going back to our roots. It is in our histories to participate in and care for our communities.

I hear all the time, "I don't know anyone who can give." Truth is, this is a dangerous myth created and perpetuated by a problematic and divisive idea of philanthropy. Plus, giving isn't only limited to moolah. It can start with donating time or other physical goods and services to your mission. When someone is intrinsically connected to your mission, in a visceral way, it becomes easier to raise funds. People want to help. They desire to give—be it a dollar or a couple hundred dollars, everyone has something to contribute, and the best part, they *want* to contribute to a good cause, so why not contribute to yours? Don't limit them from experiencing the joy of giving to a cause they deeply care about.

$ DOLLAR FOR YOUR THOUGHTS

Open your workbook. We're going to get dreamy and work through some mind drama because trust me, people want to donate their time, money, and resources. Let's help you tap into it.

1. Think about why and how you got into your work. What was your driving force?
2. What are some causes you are passionate about?
3. Why are those causes important to you?
4. Think about a time you were asked to donate to a cause you cared deeply about (your time, money, or other resources).
5. At the time, were you in a position to contribute toward this cause?
6. How did donating make you feel?
7. What if you didn't get asked to donate?

CHAPTER 4

TIME TO LEAVE THE POSTAL CODE NAMED SCARCITY

It's time to move out of the scarcity mindset. The majority of us have lived there most of our lives, and yes, I know it's comfortable, familiar, and safe, but it will not help you get to where you desire to go with your mission.

Your incredibly important mission requires you to leave the neighborhood of scarcity and lack and move into one of abundance, in every way. Just because we've been told one story about philanthropy, or about ourselves as fundraisers, it doesn't have to be true. We can change the narrative.

We become what we believe in. It is so important to tackle our mindset when fundraising, and to do that without compromising our values and authenticity. I often come across clients who have incredible stories behind their missions, but they often find it hard to ask for what their mission needs, monetarily, to thrive and make the impact it's designed to create. And it boils down to two things: the limiting beliefs they've internalized and their willingness to release those beliefs and to write a new story and chart a new narrative.

"Cindy, it feels icky to ask someone to donate to (enter your mission)."

Hot tip: Fundraising isn't hard or yucky. In fact, the more we tell our brain that fundraising is difficult, our brain will continue to reinforce this notion and make you feel queasy. It's a negative reinforcing loop.

Our brain is designed to protect us from threats and harm. When the stories we've told ourselves about fundraising include that no one wants to give (therefore we are jeopardizing relationships) or that we're not good at something (therefore it takes extra work and we don't have the time) or that people we know don't have money (so we're making them uncomfortable), well, then it's easy to see why we SHOULDN'T fundraise. But those stories are just that—stories!

"Cindy, I feel like I have to be someone else to fundraise successfully. It feels like I have to sell my soul to do it right."

Hot tip: You do not have to become someone else to fundraise successfully. You only need to be you. Having a growth mindset for fundraising does not mean you need to be inauthentic or sell out your values and mission. In fact, these beliefs are often a terrible hangover from the idea that philanthropy only comes from the wealthy, so we have to contort ourselves into someone else who can connect with these "other" wealthy people. Pretending to be someone else when fundraising is exhausting, and no one can sustain that in the long term. And yes, it does feel like you've sold your soul when you can't be yourself.

Much of our mindset for scarcity or abundance has been wired the way it is because of what we experienced, heard, or saw growing up (again, it's that repetition like learning to walk).

"Charities shouldn't have overhead."
"Fundraising is asking people to do something they don't want to do."
"People will be offended if we ask them for money."
"Only rich people give."
"Money is taboo, and we shouldn't talk about it."

Believe me, I have heard it all and I want to help you shift out of this negative reinforcement loop and write a new one. One that feels limitless, full of possibilities. What if we approached this differently? What if we rekindle the spark that once had us so deeply ignited about our mission?

I want you to start to flesh out and uncover some of your fundraising beliefs. For example, here are some things people say to me all the time:

- *Fundraising is begging.*
- *Fundraising is icky.*
- *We should ask corporations because they have money.*
- *Grants are so much easier.*
- *We don't want to grow our individual giving because maintaining those relationships is too hard and too much work.*
- *This person has so much money that they SHOULD just give it to us.*
- *We can't ask our community to give because they don't have money.*
- *It's too hard to explain what we do.*
- *It feels wrong when there are so many other pressing issues going on in the world.*
- *We just need to find a few donors with big pockets.*
- *We just need one board member who can fundraise.*
- *If we ask for too much, does it look like we are greedy?*
- *We don't see value in focusing on donors who give less than $10,000.*
- *Everything we send has to look professional and sleek to make us look legitimate and deserving to funders and donors.*

I want you to pause for a moment and identify your fundraising beliefs. They can be negative or positive. Neither is right or wrong. These are beliefs that have been ingrained within us through our upbringing, experiences, and of course, what we heard around us growing up. These are the beliefs that creep up quietly or maybe you're not even aware of them until now. These beliefs should bring up emotions for you. Beliefs are tied to feelings.

For example, if you believe that fundraising is overwhelming, you might feel incapable or like you are not a strong leader.

If your belief is that you're not good at fundraising, maybe you feel like you don't have anything in common with your donors.

If you believe fundraising is sleazy, maybe you feel like money is something that divides people. Or you were taught to not talk about money growing up.

I want you to go ahead and write down some of the feelings that come up around these beliefs. There is literally no one watching, so take your time and really think about it. Dig into your feelings and beliefs.

Now, I want you to think about where these beliefs came from.

As I described, those shortcuts in your brain are wired over time through repetitive thoughts. What has repeated itself in your life or career that has led to those beliefs?

Is it that you're constantly being told: "We're not in it for the money."

Have you had really awkward experiences around fundraising?

Were you brought up to believe that money is not something you should talk about?

Or that money is the root of all evil?

I want you to take a few minutes with this. The answers should not be obvious. If they were obvious, we'd be more aware of them day-to-day. They show up for you as fact. As truth. As reality.

We hold on to these things because they make us feel safe. We develop beliefs to protect us, so it's very scary to let them go.

So often, we feel like fundraising success is a factor of the external environment and not a result of our mindset, habits, and practices. But nothing could be further from the truth. Your mindset will carry you through almost everything in life. Do you get where I am going with this? Henry Ford said it best, "Whether you think you can or you think you can't—you're right!"

I get it, often when we're working in smaller organizations, it feels like what we do doesn't always matter. That there are all these external forces that have predetermined our success. And because we feel that it doesn't matter, things don't change. As a result, we stop trying, we stop believing that we can affect change. It then feels like a monotonous chore instead of a path we were once very passionate about. And then it becomes a self-fulfilling prophecy. The negative loop continues.

There were a few studies conducted by a psychologist named Julian B. Rotter on what he called the locus of control in personality, whereby the center of control is the degree to which people believe that they have control over the outcome of events in their lives, as opposed to external forces beyond their control. This means that those people with an internal locus of control believe that they're responsible for their own fates and that success is a function of hard work. On the other end of this continuum are those who believe in an external locus of control, often feeling like they are powerless and that life is happening *to* them, instead of *for* them. That their life is a direct result of their circumstances and there is nothing they can do about it. And the reality is, what we believe in is what we think, and what we think often indicates the state of our life and anything else as a result. *Both people are right, because of their beliefs and thoughts. The difference? One believes in personal power and responsibility, while the other hands their personal power away and believes in circumstantial power.*

Those who believe in an internal center of control, work hard and determine their success. They outperform others because they own their outcomes. Even when things don't work out due to external factors beyond their control, they focus on improving and growing themselves. They focus on learning, growth, opportunities, and the lessons within each experience as a means to do better next time. Those who believe in an external locus of control, don't try. They don't do the work that is required, and as a result, they are not successful. Which then leads to them not showing up.

Both internal and external locus of control become self-fulfilling prophecies. And when we don't own our outcomes or take full responsibility for things, we teach ourselves that it doesn't matter what we do. So we stop doing the things that matter. We reinforce the dialogue that it is okay to let ourselves and others down.

So let's be realistic. You are not going to show up 100 percent of the time in all the perfect ways that I described. You will have days when you feel hopeless. You will have days when you encounter one setback after the next. But the one thing you can do consistently? Keep showing up. Keep going. No matter what. Come back to this. Return to the mindset work.

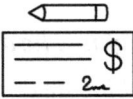

BONUS CHECK FOR YOUR FUNDRAISING SUCCESS

- **Align your mindset first, then build habits and tactics.** No matter how many tactics you learn for fundraising, if you're putting on the brakes (i.e., using a negative mindset), you're not going to get the results you want. Align your mindset first, then lean into the tools and tactics.
- **Give your brain space to change.** The more you force yourself to change, the harder it is to change. That's a natural survival mechanism. So when trying to create new pathways of thinking for your brain, be patient with yourself and set aside self-judgments.
- **Stay true to your values.** One of the biggest turning points for many of my students is gaining the understanding that their values and mission are what inspire funders and donors to support them. So stay true to your values as you align your mindset for fundraising success.

CHAPTER 5

ACTION WILL GET YOU PLACES WHERE IDEAS WON'T

There are two types of people who join my programs or work with me and my team at The Good Partnership.

There are the people who show up, do the work, and see progress. And there are the people who dismiss certain steps of the process or think they're "too busy" to get all the work done. So they don't. And their fundraising doesn't change.

Hot tip: Action will get you to places where ideas won't. I love ideas just as much as any other person. I think they're important and they ignite passion, hope, and ambition within each of us. But there is something more important to remember—the best ideas are the ones that get executed.

How many of you reading this likely have a notebook filled with ideas, goals, and dreams that haven't yet seen the light of day? Exactly my point. To paraphrase Brené Brown, you have to show up in the arena.

You have to be willing to show up for your vision, your mission, and your cause that you care deeply about—no matter your title within the organization. The best leader is often the one who has no title but shows up like the leader they know they are. Leadership comes in all packages, in all personalities. Lead yourself and your team into action, and if you find yourselves stuck, take a moment to pause, assess the gaps, understand the root cause, and do the emotional work to get yourselves unstuck so you can keep going.

We love ideas but don't take action. We continue to throw money at the problem by hiring high-priced consultants, paying for a fundraising strategy, or hiring before fixing, instead of resolving the underlying issues such as boosting self and team morale, managing emotions, and rewiring our internal beliefs to align with our mission's values and vision. I get that everyone feels busy, but the reality is that how we spend our time is a clear indication of what we enjoy doing and what we think is a priority.

I often see Executive Directors wearing all the hats, even when they have a team (of one or more) to help with the load. Part of this is a lack of trust in their teams (yes, I said it); the other part boils down to a white-knuckle grip on maintaining control and overseeing every little detail. The ED often then ends up becoming the manager who is ensuring that everything that needs to get done actually does get done. Meanwhile, they really need to be out there at the forefront, connecting with more people, building relationships, sharing the ideas that get tossed around in the boardroom over the bagels and coffee. Yet they find themselves stuck in managing the nuts and bolts of the whole operation, along with playing referee to team dynamics and politics. I am generalizing here, but you see where I am going with this. And often, this circles back to the roadblocks and limiting beliefs the EDs themselves also have about fundraising. And the vicious cycle or never-ending loop continues, and as a result, the whole organization suffers. The truth is, nobody is ever too busy to do the inner work because the inside often reflects the outside. For change to occur on the outside, it first has to occur within.

What I've observed working in our sector, working with a lot of small nonprofits and charities, is that so much of our day-to-day work is not actually helping us move forward toward our goals. A lot of it is inertia and just making sure we keep things running. We do things because that's the way they've always been done, or we get into routines that have lost their efficacy. Where we spend our time isn't always where we need to spend our time.

I was once contacted by an organization who was panicking because their fundraising was in decline and they wanted help and advice on how they could stop the boat from sinking, so to speak. The ED felt completely overwhelmed by the pressure to raise money and the need for funds just to keep the lights on. She was losing sleep, and the future of the organization was in jeopardy. When I looked at their historical fundraising revenue, it was clear that direct mail had been a big generator of income for them. So, I asked why they hadn't sent an appeal in over a year. Can you guess the response?

"I'm too busy," the Executive Director responded.

There was literally a clear path forward for the organization to raise money (proven, even!), but the ED couldn't break out of her daily cycle to just get it done. And the benefit—raising the money she needed to stop the worry and keep the organization afloat—was worth more than almost anything else she could spend her time on. On top of that, I can't tell you how many hours she spent wringing her hands with worry, too distracted to do other work.

I wish I could tell you that this was unique. But it's far from that. I see this with organizations over and over again, especially with reluctant fundraisers.

I'm going to share with you here the **Eisenhower Matrix**—an incredibly useful tool that can help you understand the value of your time so you can start taking action on the things that matter most. The Eisenhower Matrix has two axes: time and level of importance. Let's examine the different quadrants.

First, we have **DO**. These are things that are urgent and important. Things that are nonnegotiable with your time, that are moving things forward in a material and meaningful way. They are also most suited to your role.

For example, something like payroll might be critical, but is that really the best use of an Executive Director's or CEO's time? Does it move forward the big scary goals that you have? Does it add value? Not really. In fact, that might better fall into the delegate quadrant. Instead, think of this as your board engagement, big grant submissions, or reporting. These are the things that when they come up, you jump to accommodate.

Quadrant 2 is **SCHEDULE**. Think of this as that to-do list you have that always seems to keep growing, and nothing seems to get checked off. In fact, you have lists about various lists. It makes me feel overwhelmed even thinking of that. Things on your schedule quadrant are things that have been on your to-do list for a long time that are important, but it's almost too overwhelming to get started. You realize it's important and needs to get done, but you've procrastinated or put it off as long as you can. And sometimes, it just never gets done until it's urgent in neon red lights. These could be things such as fundraising, strategic planning, and grant writing (submitted on the minute it's due).

Quadrant 3 is **DELEGATE**. Let's face it, many of our organizations don't have anyone to delegate to, so I have decided to rename or customize Quadrant 3 to **BATCH**. Batching is a habit where you schedule time to do small, menial tasks all together, as a batch, instead of having them creep into the rest of your time. But if you can delegate, delegate. I know so many organizations won't apply to hire a summer intern or hire a new grad because training them and getting them up to speed feels like more work than just doing it themselves. And while that is true and can take anywhere from three to six months for a new team member to find their groove, you'll be so happy you delegated the things that really don't light you up or aren't of your expertise. If you have no one to delegate to at the moment, start blocking off time in your calendar every day or week to manage things such as email, calendars, booking appointments, payroll, website updates, social media, podcasting, etc.

Last but not least, and probably one of my favorites, is Quadrant 4, **ELIMINATE**. I want you, nope, scratch that, I *need* you to take a good hard look at what you're doing and ask yourself if it really needs to get done. This is the hardest quadrant of the four because it requires us to get honest with ourselves. It will also highlight all the time-wasters in our day, and it is highly likely that you spend the majority of your day working on the things in Quadrant 4 instead of the other three. For example, I list social media in this category. To me, it's not important to be on ALL social media platforms. Instead of five platforms, choose the two platforms that are most relevant to your audience and go all in on them. You'll notice a massive difference in your engagement, connection, and community. Eliminate the others.

I get it, ideas, action, and time management go hand in hand. You cannot spend time executing your ideas if you are spending time on TikTok trying to create fundraising videos. I want you to be intentional with your time, your execution of ideas, and take ownership of it.

Your best ideas are waiting for you to show up to them, but you cannot do so unless you've taken ownership of your time. Ideas need space and creativity and then tons of messy action to see the best ones through. None of which is possible unless you understand where you need to focus, delegate, or eliminate. And getting into messy action typically helps you arrive at crystal clear clarity faster than sitting around in a boardroom writing ideas on a wall. Everyone wants to eat, but few will do what it takes to make sure the table always has food on it.

($) DOLLAR FOR YOUR THOUGHTS

We are going to roll up our sleeves and get right into the nitty-gritty. Grab your workbook and pen. It's time to be honest about your time (pun intended!). Let's help you create time and space to execute your best ideas. Start by keeping track of your time in the Eisenhower Matrix. Just for a week or two. See where you are spending time. Then, create your ideal Eisenhower Matrix and pick just a few actions you can take regularly to move you from where you are right now to your ideal. You won't get there overnight, but start small and be consistent.

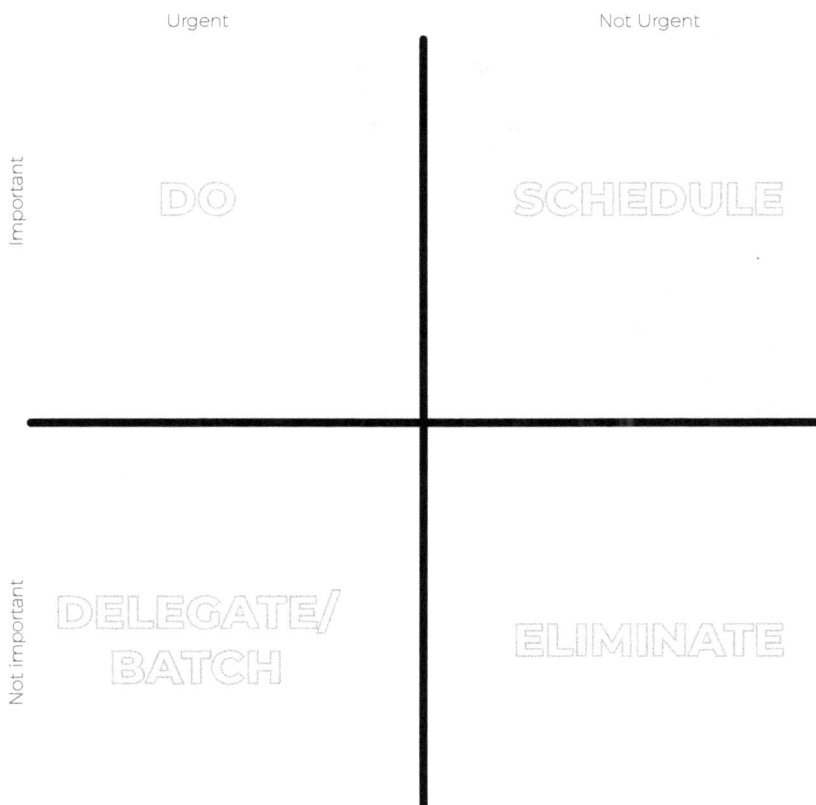

	Urgent	Not Urgent
Important	DO	SCHEDULE
Not important	DELEGATE/ BATCH	ELIMINATE

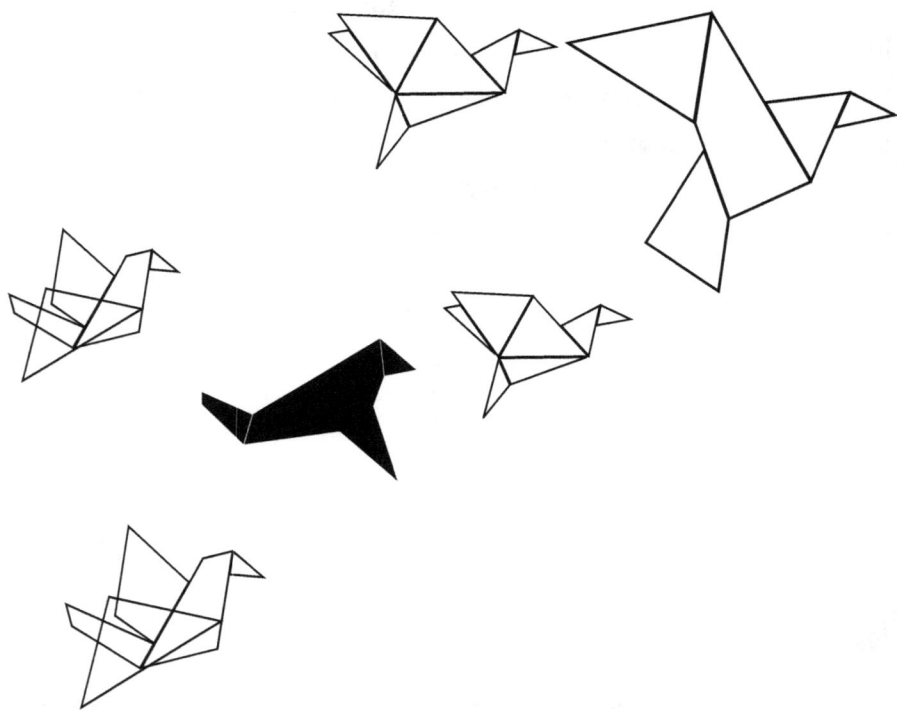

SECTION 2

LET'S REWIRE YOUR BRAIN! WOO-HOO!

This is the hill that I will die on. You are only as successful as your mindset (aka neural pathways).

Now that you know the shortcuts in your brain govern your behavior, it is the time to start to identify those existing shortcuts and rewire them toward successful fundraising.

Every successful fundraiser has mastered their mindset and is always looking for growth opportunities that help grow both themselves and their missions.

You know that your brain has pathways (like driving routes), but I have another analogy for you. Our mind is a lot like a garden. Whatever we feed it is what takes root and grows as a result. Our thoughts, behaviors, language, and the people around us all play a crucial role in helping us shape our mindset. Remember, those pathways are formed by repetition. However, we are the ones who hold the power and ability to choose who and what we surround ourselves with.

There is a saying that I keep seeing online: "You cannot change the people around you, but you can change the people around you." Makes you think, doesn't it?

This means that while you cannot change people, you can certainly change who you choose to be around and who you let inside your head. Whose advice you take, who you allow to influence your thoughts, actions, decisions as a result. We are conditioned to function on autopilot, without ever questioning anything.

For instance, I love ice cream (I mean, who doesn't, right?). But I love, LOVE ice cream. I could eat it every meal of every day. I come by it naturally—my mom also loves ice cream. And now my kids have followed suit.

I especially love ice cream when I'm stressed. If you put a salad and a bowl of ice cream in front of me when I'm stressed (and let's face it, even when I'm not), I'm 100 percent choosing the ice cream over the greens. I don't think I could muster enough willpower ever to decide to eat a salad over ice cream.

But it's not my fault! I haven't cultivated the habit of choosing the salad, nor have I seen anything different done around me.

Behaviors and actions are almost always a result of a sequence that looks like the one I just described above.

"Because it's always been done this way . . . " is something I hear often enough, but that is no excuse to stay stagnant and hinder the growth of your mission. And growth first starts with you, *within* you.

How many times have you talked yourself out of personal and professional growth because it seemed daunting, hard, and overwhelming? Now, those are the times you're aware of, but imagine how many times your brain is preventing you from things without you even knowing!

On the flip side, how many times have you attempted something in earnest and been surprised at how much you've enjoyed it once you taught yourself something new and paired that with discipline and consistency? This is because you rewired a brain pattern. It likely took you about three weeks to form the habit and more like ten weeks (70 days) to find your own rhythm of comfort and consistency.

So imagine the possibilities if you can continuously focus on growth and learning new habits.

In this section, I'm going to walk you through the process to rewire your brains to fundraising success. It starts with some awareness (we have to uncover these decisions our brains are making on autopilot), followed by an understanding of habits (again, repetition), and finally, we'll look at some practical ways you can create new shortcuts in your brain.

Before we dig in, here are some hard truths that you likely need to hear:

1. You know what you need to do, but it's often fear that holds you back. Fear of what others think. Fear of the unknown. Fear of doing hard things.
2. Emotional intelligence and genuine relationship building will open more doors for you than any one-size-fits-all strategy.

3. Reluctance breeds reluctance. Your energy and mindset attracts and propels forward the right opportunities of growth for you.
4. Growth requires you to get uncomfortable.
5. Repetition, consistency, and discipline will persist when motivation and passion fade.

As much as we often scoff at the soft skills that are essential to our personal and professional growth and development, they are needed. Gone are the days of trying to be anyone else but yourself. It's time to let your personality shine through and own your strengths while refining the areas you find yourself a bit wobbly in. This section will help you identify your feelings, beliefs, and values that you possess and other values that you might want to harness and develop. And this section will help you understand exactly how to rewire your mindset, reframe old narratives, and develop successful habits that will last a lifetime, as long as you are willing to do the work.

CHAPTER 6

WHAT TYPE OF FUNDRAISER ARE YOU?

I love asking people that question because believe it or not, everyone has a type. I don't know about you, but I love personality tests (I fully blame Buzzfeed)—anything that helps me know and understand myself and those around me better gets my vote! Just like a character in a movie or a good book, we all tend to resemble a few personas—and the same applies in fundraising.

I didn't coin the term "Reluctant Fundraiser" out of thin air. It came about as an astute observation after numerous conversations with incredible individuals who had inspiring and heart-centered missions, but they felt reluctant to go shout them from the rooftops and enroll the support they needed. Now this isn't to say that all people responsible for fundraising (I would call them fundraisers, but many don't identify as such) are reluctant. Some of them just need a little bit of help owning their greatness, while others need deeper support so they can go out and connect with their communities and rally more support for their missions. Some of them get stuck in the vicious cycle that is perfectionism, and others are still healing and rewiring their beliefs around money, self-worth, and more. Wherever you fall on the Reluctant Fundraiser spectrum, it's totally okay. In fact, you may find that you don't actually fit into any of these, and that's okay too. I still want you to think about the feelings and beliefs that come up for you as you think about fundraising so you can build awareness of those mental shortcuts that might be unique to you. As you read through each of the archetypes, I want you to make a mental note of how you feel when you read each description. Notice what stands out to you most and what resonates with you. Let's take you from reluctant fundraiser to fundraising superhero.

I've worked with a lot of organizations and a lot of people, and I've created four buckets for reluctant fundraising archetypes.

I am going to walk you through what some of the most common beliefs around fundraising are. These are typical mindset dialogues that we need to shift by rewiring the neural pathways in our brains. For each archetype, I have created an alter ego or super power that you can tap into if it resonates. Doing so will help you be more productive and help you move toward greater success in fundraising. Ready? I know you can't tell me you're ready, but I'm gonna assume you're ready. Let's go.

THE PERFECTIONIST

The first archetype is what I call the **Perfectionist**. And chances are, you're either running your organization, are on the board of directors, or are in your position because you're really good at certain work, right? Having worked in the sector for a long time, I've noticed that we're good at promoting people internal to our organizations. I've seen so many frontline or subject matter experts get promoted to the role of Executive Director, and with good reason. We often recruit board members because they have legal skills or HR skills. These are skills that we possess based on experience, education, and of course, what comes naturally to us. We are really good at it and comfortable doing what is required of us. It's second nature.

Contrary to that, and for the most part, we are not taught to fundraise, so we're not good at it. That doesn't mean we cannot master it and become an expert at it. Because guess what, learning to do hard things takes time and practice. And so, while you might not classify yourself as a perfectionist, you might find yourself saying things like, "I just need the right plan." I also hear this quite often from board members, "Just tell me what to do," and in some cases, I hear the opposite, "Here are tons of ideas. Let me tell you what to do. I'm going to focus on the ideation instead of the implementation." These are both signs that this individual is a perfectionist. It plays into the dialogue so prevalent in our sector, "We would pretty much rather stay in our lane because that's what we're good at, not fundraising." To that I say, bullshit (sorry, but I'm super passionate about this!). You are good at fundraising, you just haven't mastered the art. Yes, fundraising is an art and a science blended together.

To give you an example, I was having coffee with a friend a couple summers back, and we were talking about yoga. And I confess, I'm not a fan of yoga, it's just not my thing. I really like to focus on proper posture. And I have a hard time doing that. And keeping up with the pace usually means that I basically end up twisted into a heap of limbs in the corner. So my friend who is a yoga enthusiast said something to me that I'll never forget:

"Can you stick with being bad at something long enough to get good at it?" Mind blowing, right?! And that is the exact question I want you to ask yourself, especially if the archetype of the Perfectionist resonates with you.

We learn by doing because no one's taught us how to talk about money with people, or you know how to fundraise or cultivate an engaged community. This is why we need to practice consistently and master the things we need to do that are inherent to our missions and the impact they create. I've lovingly named your alter ego—if you're the Perfectionist—the **Doer**. What the Doer does, instead of learning more, hiring more, and waiting for all the answers to come to them, they go out and find them. They put in the effort—big and small action steps—to make it happen. After all, success is defined by your efforts. So try this and just do the damn thing. Messy action will beat perfect inaction any day!

THE WOUNDED

I call this archetype the **Wounded** because they get chills when the word "fundraising" is even mentioned. It feels paralyzing—stopping them dead in their tracks. And for some others, it can feel like an old wound has quite literally been opened, and now it's aching and hurting all over the place. Hence my name for it. This archetype takes fundraising very personally. They almost always make every rejection mean something about them.

Can I ask for money? What if the person says no? Won't that make things awkward between us? How will I talk to them again after that? Sound familiar? You're not alone. I see you.

The fear of rejection is too big to overcome for the Wounded. Fundraising is essentially something that falls to the back burner. It's a nonstarter. And the thought of being told "no" can feel like a personal rejection. *What did I do wrong? Why was I not good enough? Why don't they think our work is worth it?*

And then we see that person or corporation give to another similar organization, we start doubting ourselves even more. *What is it about me that they wouldn't give to us, but clearly they care because they could give to that other organization?* Raise your hand if you've ever thought that. I know I have.

The Wounded take to heart when a donor does not or cannot donate to their mission.

If you identify with this persona, say hello to your alter ego: the **Visionary**. The Visionary is the community builder. Think of all the ways you can leverage this alter ego, especially if you or your board members resonate with the Wounded. The Visionary brings people together, over a shared vision. They build a meaningful buy-in, they listen to one another, and they turn feedback into connection. They mobilize support so people say "yes" before they're even asked (yes, that happens).

As leaders, Visionaries unite their people and enable and empower them to contribute in ways they can. The focus is not on the ask. As the Visionary, make it your mission to connect with people and not talk about money during your conversation. I know this might sound strange at first, and perhaps you are secretly thanking me for saying this because it feels more comfortable for you. Genuine, human connection instead of going right for the ask. Yes, fundraising can be this simple. Connect with people, without any expectations, without focusing on money, at least for the first little while. Call up your donors, treat them to a virtual coffee, get to know them.

During my time as an in-house fundraiser, no matter where I worked, I would always make it my personal mission to connect with our donors and our staff. It was important to me to understand why our donors supported us and why our staff continued to work as hard as they do. And once I understood those things, it felt easy to mobilize people around this shared vision and get them excited and feeling good about giving. Get to know your community, that's where the magic truly is. Once you understand why they care and build deeper relationships with them, you will experience fundraising to be a lot easier.

Quick caveat: I often get asked this question, "What if our donors give because they are asked by our board, ED, or staff person, and only give because of that relationship? They are giving to support the person, not the cause." While this may be true (and we've all done this at one point or another), remember that this is an opportunity to then see if these donors really do care about the cause and how can you bring them closer to it?

Remember, fundraising isn't about giving to us personally. It's about giving to a cause that might be close to our heart, giving to a cause whose mission we feel intrinsically connected to. We're trying to find the people who connect with our mission, our impact. Fundraising success comes from building a strong vision, and from getting people to buy in for that vision and mobilizing people around our mission.

THE IDEALIST

Our next archetype is a personal favorite of mine because I tend to see this a lot in our industry, especially working with social justice-based organizations. We have been taught to view the world in dichotomies. The us versus them, good versus bad, and right versus wrong. This is how our society has been built traditionally. It is easier to understand and function in our world that way (hello, mental shortcut!).

I would call this archetype the **Idealist**, though there are more nuances to it. For the Idealist, fundraising is all about dichotomies. They have a hard time dismantling the idea of philanthropy. Often there is a good versus bad mentality, the haves versus the have-nots. It then becomes a matter of typecasting; the ones with the money are the only ones who can be philanthropists. The Idealist is uncomfortable with the idea of philanthropy because to them, the question always becomes who do I know who can give to this mission in a way where we're not selling our soul? They can't picture anyone they know who can write a check for $10,000, so they feel like they don't know anyone who "can" give.

Traditionally, people who have lots of money have been the gatekeepers and in control over giving it to important social change work. And this power imbalance is deeply problematic. We cannot fund meaningful change this way. I built my whole fundraising career on this premise. But the problem is, governments are not always reliable, and foundations are giving out a lot of money, but often in a way that is upholding the status quo. Naturally, the Idealist is forced to turn to fundraising, but it feels uncomfortable, like they are being asked to sell their soul. So, if you resonate with this archetype, at some point in your fundraising career (especially if you are in a social justice or community-based organization) you've thought the following:

> *We don't know anyone with money.*
> *Who's going to donate to us?*
> *What if this goes against everything we stand for?*
> *What if I have to abandon my values?*

My question to you is: How are you supposed to fundraise if you have no donors? And how are you supposed to find donors if they're not in your world, if you don't already know wealthy people? Most organizations answer this with: "Okay, how do we get in front of that wealthy individual, corporation, or foundation?" Or you focus on things like government funding and grants (government and corporate) because it feels safer and aligns with your values.

However, we still need to fundraise. And while I am all for applying for grants, etc., you cannot pin the future of your mission on a chance that you might win a grant. This is why it's important to embrace fundraising with open arms.

Fundraising doesn't mean compromising your values. It should enhance and enable your mission, not work against it. And the more we start to understand that it's not up to us to decide who has money and who can make a donation, the more we'll see that, in fact, the act of giving and having control over the impact you want to see on the world is an empowering act in itself. Fun fact: I wrote my university thesis on this topic almost 20 years ago, and it's more relevant now than ever!

Fundraising, at its core, has always been about mobilizing community and connecting people with the causes they care about. And no matter what anyone tells you, cause will always come before the dollar.

As an organization, you cannot be reliant on one or two big funders. If the pandemic taught us anything, it's that we need community support, because if something happens to one big funder or they redirect their giving focus, it can hurt and destabilize your organization.

There is no right or wrong strategy with fundraising. You have to find the strategy that works for you and your organization. So, if you are the Idealist, and you are preventing yourself from getting into fundraising or from being more effective in fundraising because of the earlier mentioned beliefs, I want you to tap into the alter ego of the **Connector**. The Connector connects with their community—regardless of the outcome. They are genuinely interested in understanding community needs and desires. They tap into the *why*. So connect with your supporters (even if they don't always donate) and with your donors who are giving smaller amounts. Whether it's a donor who contributes $10 each month or the donor who has been giving you $50 a year for the past five years, it matters. To them. To you. To your mission. I want you to understand *why* those people continue to give to your cause. What is it that makes it meaningful to them? Because if you can understand that, you will be able to zero in on your community and easily attract your supporters.

THE ACROBAT

And finally, say hello to the **Acrobat**, a personal favorite because a lot of small organization EDs fall into this category. You can almost picture it—walking the tightrope, contorting themselves into all elaborate positions of a Cirque du Soleil star. This is what it's like running a small organization or you know, fundraising—no matter if you are a small or mid-sized organization. The work in our sector can feel like we have to be an acrobat, and burnout is the medal that we win for all the feats we accomplish or die trying to accomplish. To an extent, it feels like it's part of the package. That this is what you get when you sign up to work in the charitable sector or are a small business that is also mission-driven and heart-led—underpaid, overworked, and underappreciated, with barely any time to brush your teeth, let alone manage the fundraising. For some twisted reason, we think this way of working is okay because it comes with the territory. But it's not okay. Our work is far too important to die at the altar of burnout or to sit on the sidelines because we are wearing all the hats and doing all the things.

This is why fundraising for the Acrobat feels daunting and nothing ever gets done—it feels impossible compared to the urgent things that need to get done. Nobody is coming to save you or your mission. Your impact needs to matter more to you than the ability to hold on to control by doing all the things.

Things are never complete, and there is always so much to do. I get it. That's the nature of trying to change the world! Just as you cross a few things off your list, it's like the list magically had twenty more things added to it. This vicious cycle continues until you are ready to surrender wholeheartedly to the fact that you and your organization are here to create the impact of a lifetime, instead of the overnight success express (which never works anyway!). Lasting social change takes place over years. While it may start with you and even be led by you, the impact or the ripple effect will be felt across the years. So how can you find balance and harmony in this chaos? Say hello to your alter ego, the **Harmonizer.**

The Harmonizer is an excellent maestro and knows how to organize what would otherwise sound like a cacophony into a harmonious symphony. They know that they need to focus on and prioritize what matters most, while delegating the rest. They don't multitask. They focus on the task at hand and turn off all distractions. Hyper focus equals hyper speed and precision. Even if it is one hour a week that is spent on the one thing that they need to do to move the needle. Think of the impact that allows them to create as a fundraiser. And they also understand that delegation means that change and growth come from being consistent with best practices. And most of all, they forgive themselves and their team when things get messed up; after all, that's where learning happens.

Whew, that was quite a bit to chew on. I invite you to reread this chapter and come back to it throughout your fundraising journey. You might even find that you start out with one archetype and have evolved into another. Wherever you find yourself, know this: As long as you lead with authenticity, you will win over far more supporters and donors than any strategy would. Your impact matters. You matter. Your mission matters. Start dedicating time to understanding yourself more and those around you so that together you can create a ripple effect across the globe, across time.

$ DOLLAR FOR YOUR THOUGHTS

With your pen and workbook ready, we are going to go on a date with your archetypes and alter egos. Time to get really honest, raw, and vulnerable with yourself.

1. Which archetype resonated the most with you, at this moment? Why?
2. Which alter ego resonated with you? Why?
3. Keeping in mind the archetype and the alter ego that resonated with you, what are some things that you tend to avoid with fundraising? You can be honest.
4. What are some things within fundraising that you are naturally good at? How often do you spend time doing that?
5. What is one thing you are committed to mastering?
6. What is one thing you are committed to delegating?
7. Why does your mission matter to you? Yes, I know I am asking this again. Because repetition is key and keeping your mission front and center will get rid of any *what ifs, thens, and buts.*

CHAPTER 7

STOP TRIPPING OVER YOUR TRIGGERS

Identifying our archetypes and alter egos is all fun and games until we run into what I like to call chain reactions . . . and what many others like to call triggers. Given that our brain prefers to take the easier way out and rewiring our neural pathways to change our behaviors and developing new patterns can take up to 70 days, consider this chapter your mini cheat sheet.

We now know that we develop fundraising beliefs and feelings over time, which secretly create shortcuts in our brains to then control our fundraising behavior. We need to understand how these beliefs show up for us and how they affect our fundraising results.

I want you to gain awareness of how these beliefs do or do not align with where you want your organization to grow and how you want to grow as a fundraiser. Do they serve the legacy you want to create?

Here's what happens in our brains as we go through the world: Circumstances —> beliefs —> feelings —> actions —> results.

If we want to change our results, we have to change the sequence that leads to them.

There are circumstances, or triggers, that happen—which is basically us engaging with the world around us. Triggers that cause the chain reaction can be interactions, events, conversations, etc. I want you to take a minute to identify your fundraising triggers, good and bad. These are the circumstances that come up in your day-to-day activities where these beliefs and emotions surface.

For example, maybe a trigger is when fundraising comes up on the agenda at the board meeting. Or you're at an event. Or sitting at your computer trying to write a note to a donor. Perhaps you feel triggered reading this book or maybe it's from listening to a podcast on fundraising or being around family and friends who don't quite understand why you do what you do for a living.

This is where I want you to slow down and pay attention, try and catch yourself in the moment. When that trigger occurs, what is the first thought that pops up in your mind? What are the emotions that arise for you? This is the part that we're not usually aware of, so I want you to pause and think.

Sometimes, these beliefs or thoughts can be totally irrational. In fact, most times they are irrational, but they show up as a truth for you. These beliefs are developed through our survival instincts; in that moment, it feels like our whole world could collapse. In retrospect, it is totally silly. It could be that you believe you have nothing in common with your donors. Or that you're going to look foolish or unqualified and feel embarrassed because you don't have answers to questions that are being asked of you. Sometimes, we can best identify these when we give advice to others. Oftentimes, we're really good at giving advice but terrible at following our own advice. Ask yourself, do I practice what I preach? If not, then you need to change this trigger sequence.

Here's an example of a sequence I see come up again and again. I always recommend (over and over again, in fact) that individuals book meetings with their donors and supporters (individuals, corporations, foundations) to get to know them and find out why they support your organization. There is no ask in these meetings—it's just a chance to listen and learn. It doesn't matter HOW MANY TIMES I repeat this advice, most reluctant fundraisers never get started. They never send that email or pick up that phone. Here's what that sequence might look like:

- Circumstance: You learn that without a doubt, one of the most effective actions you can take with fundraising (especially mission-centered fundraising) is to get to know your supporters.

- Belief: Your brain is slamming on the breaks. *I believe that I'm not experienced enough or don't know the "right" way to manage these meetings. I believe I can't be authentic, and I have to present myself in a way that is uncomfortable or not "me."*

- Feelings: *I feel nervous and anxious and like an impostor. I'm questioning my leadership whether I'm even the right person to be fundraising.*

- Actions: *I just don't do the work. I focus on something else that is more comfortable.*

- Results: *I don't get to know my donors, and therefore I can't ask them to give in a meaningful way, so our fundraising isn't as effective, and we're not raising as much money as we could be.*

Think about this for a moment and write down all the beliefs that come up or tie the triggers back to the beliefs you've already identified through the journal prompts in prior chapters.

Feelings are the emotions that accompany your beliefs. For example, they might be sad, scared, happy, nervous, angry, guilty, or ashamed.

What are the emotions that come up for you as you read this? Write them down.

This is where the magic takes place. When those brain shortcuts really kick into high gear—Action!

When we get to the action stage of the sequence or chain, we are typically unaware that we're taking action or sometimes it's inaction. For example, we might avoid what we most need to do by focusing on something else on our list that feels more comfortable or easier. We might need to really connect with our donors and make donor calls, but instead, we are planning our social media strategy or writing thank you letters or planning a gala. But it's the direct phone or face-to-face communication with our donors that will in fact spread word of our mission and help us raise funds for it.

Let's face it. There's always something else you could be doing with your time. And usually, those things can feel pretty important, easier, and certainly more comfortable. This is the inertia I mentioned earlier.

Another example is that you might go into a conversation talking too much instead of listening. Instead of allowing your potential supporter or donor to share more about themselves. Learning to actively listen helps you to understand their *why* and their connection to your mission. If you don't actively listen, you miss that opportunity by coming on too strong into the conversation by dominating all the talk time.

Or perhaps you focus on preparing and planning for every little scenario because you're not ready.

What action or inaction shows up for you? And where? Write that down.

Of course, when we do these things, it affects our results. And our mission's bottom line.

Here's another common example:

- Circumstance: *I have the opportunity to talk to someone about our organization.*

- Belief: *People don't naturally want to support our work, so I have to pitch them hard. That means we need a stellar elevator pitch and pitch deck, which we don't have.*

- Feeling: *Our organization is less impressive or this person won't want to support us because we are missing this key piece of the fundraising pie.* (Side note: You absolutely do not need an elevator pitch or pitch deck.)

- Actions: *I put off scheduling the meeting until I feel we are "ready"* (which is basically never).

- Results: *We lost that opportunity for support.*

You do not need a polished elevator pitch (a short and snappy explanation of your nonprofit that you can easily spout in the time it takes for a short elevator ride) or pitch deck (a slightly longer, written version of your elevator pitch in a marketing form used for any and all correspondence about your nonprofit). Actually, I would argue that in most circumstances, a pitch deck will do you more harm than good if you don't connect with the prospective donor first, do some good listening, and find the areas of alignment with your mission before you think about what the right pitch would be for them. And instead of an elevator pitch, try to tell a personal story that gets you emotional, one that can spark that emotion in someone else.

As a result, we fail to achieve the outcome or result we desire, and it reinforces our existing beliefs that we're bad at fundraising. Or that nobody wants to support our mission, especially if a donor doesn't donate as a result. And that becomes a self-fulfilling prophecy (I'll delve deeper into this in the next chapter). We add meaning to that sequence, instead of understanding that it's just a shortcut in our brain that we need to rewire.

> **Hot tip:** The thing with triggers and chain reactions is that the moment we gain awareness of them and understand why they occur or trigger a certain response from us, we can start to take away the power they hold over us.

While it takes practice (building habits) to change the autopilot of these sequences, we can start to identify where we need to do the work and what an alternative might look like. We no longer stop dead in our tracks or feel tongue-tied when we head into a donor meeting or are having conversations about sponsorships or grants. I always say that the strategy will help you build and grow your fundraising prowess, thereby growing your mission, but it's learning to master and understand your emotions, and to rewire your beliefs, thoughts, and behaviors that will lead to sustainable, purposeful, long-term impact and results.

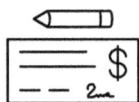

BONUS CHECK FOR YOUR FUNDRAISING SUCCESS

- **When faced with a trigger or in an environment that feels triggering, stop, drop, and ground yourself. Pause. Take a few deep breaths and anchor back into your body.** Our triggers often feel like an out-of-body experience because we are reliving a loop that occurred at different times in our life. We're on autopilot. Though we might be faced with a present set of circumstances that has activated this trigger, we approach it with layers of emotions that have been stored from the original incident that started this chain reaction. Understanding this is key. And anchoring ourselves will help us to not lose our cool or fumble with our words or freeze in our tracks.

- **When an action or inaction shows up for you, ask yourself if this is taking you closer to or further away from your fundraising mission.** Assessing things objectively helps keep us centered and focused on the cause instead of the dollar amount or the yes/no responses from donors or supporters. It helps us maintain a sense of calm and objectivity instead of taking things personally. Remember, people always meet us where they are at. And what others say or don't say—or do or don't do—is often a reflection and a result of the experiences or mind loops that they are part of (and they are likely unaware of it as well). So the only person you can control is yourself. Why not be the driving force behind your mission? And why not do it with love and community at the forefront of your mind?

CHAPTER 8

ADIOS MIND DRAMA—WE DON'T LIKE REPLAYS, JUST REWIRING

Cheeky, I know. But it's true, nobody likes replays over and over again (okay, maybe I can binge-watch *West Wing* over and over again, but that's about it). And the chain reactions that come up as a result of being faced with our triggers are just like scenes from a bad horror movie that continues to replay or hit a glitch mid-movie. Time to reset and rewire our beliefs and thought patterns so we can create new and more dominant shortcuts or pathways. This way, your brain will change your default belief, feelings, and actions, which ultimately will yield better results.

As discussed in the last chapter, we get trapped in the following sequence: Circumstances —> beliefs —> feelings —> actions —> results.

And more often than we realize, we are living life by default, instead of living by design. And the more we go through life without changing our default way of being, the deeper ingrained these become.

Rewiring our neural pathways does not have to be complicated. It might be challenging at first because you are teaching yourself a new way of being, but it is doable. And once mastered, you'll wonder why you didn't do it sooner.

By this point in the book, you perhaps have a good enough understanding of what's occurring within your mindset when it comes to fundraising. And you also have come to realize that you cannot outsmart your brain. Nobody can, at least not in the long term. The only way to outsmart your brain is by teaching it a new shortcut, a new pattern. Hello, rewiring, especially if you desire lasting, sustainable habits.

Perhaps reading some of this has brought up a few examples where you have let the mind drama take the wheel instead of being in the driver's seat yourself. I'm going to go through a few ways you can rewire your brain. You don't have to attempt these all at once, but try each one for a few minutes, and continue to build upon it (there's that habit formation again). Let's revisit the example of driving to work on autopilot. Now, let's say you're starting a new job and you have to create that new neural pathway in your brain that becomes more dominant than the old one. For the first few weeks of leaving for work, you are probably going to feel a slight pull toward your old route. If you want to make the drive to your new job the dominant route for you, you have to drive that way. Consciously at first. A lot. Until it becomes second nature for you.

But there are some other tricks you can learn around rewiring your brain, through visualization, intention, and practice. Ready to jump into all three?

REFUTE AND VISUALIZE

There have been numerous studies and research conducted to show our brains don't really know how to tell the difference between actually experiencing something and visualizing it. René Descartes summed it up in 1637 when he said, "I think therefore I am."

Imagine sitting in a movie theater watching your favorite movie. You don't even feel like you're present in your seat because you are swept away into the story. You are experiencing a complete mind-body-soul experience of the characters in the movie. Your body experiences physiological changes such as sweating or your heart pounding. To your mind, it's as if you are in the movie. It doesn't know any different or better. Now imagine what happens to your brain and the stories and narratives it continues to reinforce when you are surrounded by the same set of circumstances, people who influence or reinforce the same behavioral patterns . . . that's right, your mind continues to absorb it, and it becomes a deeply ingrained behavior—positive or negative.

In a 2013 study of pianists, scientists found that participants who mentally practiced a five-finger sequence on an imaginary piano for two hours a day had the same neurological changes (and reduction in mistakes) as the participants who physically practiced the same passage on an actual piano.

You see where I'm going with this?

If you regularly visualize a new pattern of circumstance —> beliefs —> feelings —> actions —> results, you can start to build those new pathways so they become the dominant belief.

However, it's not that easy. There is a process to this.

In your workbook that you've been taking notes in, I want you to write down those negative beliefs and feelings you have. Just record them.

Then, I want you to refute them.

That's right. We are going to refute them with logic and reasoning and solid evidence. Just like they do in the courtroom. I want you to think of rational reasons why those beliefs are wrong. I do this with my son who is scared of monsters. We think about all the rational reasons why he doesn't need to be scared. I show him pictures of the actors who play the scary monsters. We talk about how they are made up. That he's never, ever seen one in real life. And then we still check under the bed, behind the curtains, and inside the closet (tangible evidence that there are no monsters there) to reassure him that he is safe at home and can sleep without any worries.

Whatever your circumstances, beliefs, feelings, or actions are, think of examples where the opposite is true. Do you have evidence to refute your beliefs?

As I mentioned earlier, the number one thing I recommend for fund-raising is to connect with donors. Once my students get over the hump of sending that first email and they have their first meeting, it's like they are a whole new person. They just needed that one experience to prove to themselves that they were wrong.

If you're struggling with this, think about talking to someone you care about, like a close friend or colleague. What would you say to them if they came to you with the beliefs and feelings you have? We are so good at supporting others—propping them up, reassuring them, and comforting them—but we rarely do it for ourselves.

So go ahead and write all the reasons why your beliefs are wrong.

For example, let's say you're putting off booking a donor meeting because you're worried they will say no. First, you're not even asking for money! That's a great way to refute your fears. Also, your donors have already shown they care about your cause because they've already given, so it's probably likely that they do in fact want to hear from you. Finally, worst-case scenario, they say no to a meeting. So what? If they care, they are likely to keep giving and would not be put off by a friendly outreach. If they are put off and stop giving, chances are you already lost their donation well before you reached out to have a chat.

Now, I want you to practice visualizing your reality when your new beliefs are now hardwired into your brain. Ideally, open up your workbook and write this out. Write as if you are reporting back to yourself after it has already happened. For example, you can write: This morning, like all mornings, I had a 20-minute call with one of my donors and they shared the most incredible story with me about why they LOVE giving to our organization. This insight helped me better understand how to manage our social media messaging and write our next direct appeal. This one conversation turned into a meaningful opportunity to raise more money.

I want you to really feel like you are living this reality. Imagine what you can smell, see, touch, taste, etc. Transport yourself!

Then, as you go about your day, remember that you are this new person. Make decisions based on what you would do if you started your day with this amazing donor call.

🎉 IT'S GO TIME!

1. Write down your fundraising goal for this year. Just write it down. Approximation is fine. Think of this as the number that you under promise and over deliver. Write that down.

2. Next, write down your stretch goal—something that seems a little out of reach but you're going to treat yourself to something special if you reach it. This is the goal that perhaps you might not share with others, but in your heart of hearts, you know without a doubt that's what you really want to raise in funds this year. Yes, I get it, it feels a bit uncomfortable, out of reach, but there's more than enough magic available to you to get you there. Your mindset is a big part of that magic.

3. Now, double that number. Yes, you read that right. This goal should feel completely out of reach. This is your breakthrough goal. I can feel your heart racing as you do this. Don't panic. Just write down that number. This is like your wild dream. It is intentionally not achievable. I don't want you to focus on the reality of this right now. Don't

be conservative. I want you to be courageous and to just go for it. Just double the number and don't think about it.

Now, I want you to visualize how it would feel if I wrote you a check for that amount today. What would that money allow your organization to do? *And for the love of all things nonprofit, don't say hire a fundraiser. Ha!* Be focused, be ambitious, be daring! What would that money mean for the impact you desire to create? Who would it impact? How far would it go? Who could it help? How could it help? How many more people could you serve or environmental areas could you protect? What could you do with that money? This is how we dream, right?

I know this might not seem realistic, but every big mission and vision was realized and brought to fruition because one person had the courage to dream bigger and bolder than ever and just go for it. We have to be able to envision the future for our organization to create lifelong impact and change. That feels a little daring. That feels a little uncomfortable. But as Zig Ziglar so wisely said, "What you get by achieving your goals is not as important as what you become by achieving your goals."

When we have these lofty goals, the goal is not actually to get there. It's learning to become the person who can get there. Often, people focus only on the end result or outcome, without ever taking a moment to examine, understand, assess, and respect the process, the journey, the ebbs and flows. It's not about how much money you can raise (though that's what everyone wants you to think of on the surface), it's about who you become while you're in the arena, navigating the journey and raising funds.

So how do we become the person who can get there? How do we change ourselves? By building the right habits. Just like you wouldn't run a marathon without training for it consistently, rewiring your patterns and beliefs is no different. We want to train our brains for these new beliefs to become the default. This process of refuting and visualizing is part of rewiring your brain. Pretty cool, right?

FUTURE CASTING: WHO ARE YOU?

1. Visualize and write down life as your future self, that person who is raising an unimaginable amount of money. I like to call this future casting. Some people like to call this their TedTalk or their big award's acceptance speech.

2. Write it down as if you are there right now. Use the present tense, "I am . . . " instead of the future, "I will . . . "

3. Who are you? Where would you live? What time do you wake up? What's your morning routine? What are you grateful for? How do you start your day? Are you starting it with energy and hope knowing that you're going to show up for yourself and your goals and that you're going to be successful?

4. How do you feel when you go to work? If you leave the house, how do you get there? Where are you going? Where are your offices? Do you have a team? How do you greet them? How do they greet you? What does your work environment look like and feel like?

5. What's your desk like? How does your chair feel? I want you to be as descriptive as possible. Picture the colors, the textures, the smell of the office, and more. What are you spending your time doing during the day? What are your hours? How much are you actually working? What are you eating for lunch? Do you take a break?

6. How big is your organization? How many staff do you have? What do they do? What other resources do you have access to that make current challenges disappear? What new challenges come up? What problems are you solving?

7. Who are you as a leader? How are you mobilizing others to do good? And when you leave the office, what did you learn today? What did you accomplish?

8. As you unwind from your workday, what do you do? Where do you go after work? What are you grateful for? What does it feel like to end your workday? What time is it?

As you finish writing this, I want you to keep this in a place where you can read it every single day. Better yet, write it down often—again and again. I want you to keep this version of yourself in your mind as we work through the rest of this book. And every single day, I want you to focus on becoming this person now, today, this moment. In the way you move, in the way you walk, in your posture, in your conversations, in your actions, thoughts, and beliefs. Doing this every day will help rewire those neural pathways.

I know some people who do this every day or every week, but if you are unable to do it that often, promise me—more importantly, promise yourself—that you will do this at least once a month. Carve out an intentional hour or two at the beginning of each month and allow yourself to visualize, dream, and go there. Because big impact stems from big aspirations and desires, and from the courage to keep seeking it every single day.

RELEASE AND SET INTENTIONS

It's literally that. Some call it surrender; others call it an intervention; author Brendon Burchard calls it release and set intentions. This practice comes in handy any time you find yourself with the trigger or circumstance that creates an avalanche of chain reactions, beliefs, and actions.

When you find yourself in the moment, for example, before you go into a board meeting or before a donor call or before you're about to do something fundraising related, think of the specific circumstances that create your chain reaction and . . . pause. Just take two minutes.

Pause and say, "Release." Shake it off. Shake your hands, shake off that negative energy, and continue saying, "Release" until you feel that negative energy completely leave you—mind, body, and heart.

Just repeat: Release. Release. Clear. Cancel. I am not available for this any longer.

Focus on your breathing. If you're having trouble, try breathing in for three seconds and out for six, emptying your breath. Alternate nostril breathing is a technique that helps ground the nervous system and bring the awareness back to the body when our emotions are heightened or when we feel the fight/flight/freeze response that is elicited from some of our triggers.

When you feel the tension is gone, I want you to set intentions.

In your mind, come back to your journaling exercise I just walked you through and think about being that person right now. Set intentions for the situation you're about to go into. What would that person do? What would they say? How would they behave?

This is a quick way to get you back on track in those moments when it feels like the world will swallow you whole.

PRACTICE MAKES ~~PERFECT~~ PROGRESS

You know it's true, practice will help things progress faster, further, and of course, help you refine your fundraising skills. It's the best way to rewire your brain. I know, I probably sound like a broken record, but it's true!

We often overthink the actions, the doing. We worry so much about what others think, how it will land, and we busy our minds and days with tasks that don't move the needle or add to the mission's bottom line. It's no wonder we miss the mark with our fundraising goals.

Most people look at fundraisers and think, *Wow, that person is so confident, they make a great fundraiser.* Wrong! Confidence is not what predetermines your competence or success as a fundraiser.

It's the opposite. Practice, action, and the basic act of doing the thing that terrifies you is what builds confidence. It builds proof of concept. And if you want a new proof of concept, you have to master the actions day in and day out that will get you there.

As you wrap up this chapter, I want you to take a few moments and anchor in this version of yourself that you have uncovered. You've identified your beliefs, thoughts, patterns, and behavior loops that hold you back. You have already started a cascade of rewiring them by choosing to read this book and do the exercises and action steps listed in here.

I want you to anchor in gratitude—what does that feel like and look like for you? Our minds are primal and trained to focus on survival, on the what ifs, on the one thing that doesn't go right. I want you to focus on all that has gone well in your fundraising career. I want you to identify five things you are grateful for—personal and professional. And I want you to give yourself a big hug! Chin up, you've got this!

CHAPTER 9

RAISE YOUR FUNDRAISING BELIEFS TO MATCH YOUR VISION

Do your beliefs match your vision?

I ask myself this every single day. It's one way I continue to stay anchored to my mission with The Good Partnership. How do you stay connected to your mission?

As we have discovered throughout the book thus far, our deep-seated beliefs around money, fundraising, even our ability to connect with others or accomplish great things are often reinforced positively or negatively by those around us—people, situations, circumstances, interactions, etc.

Eventually this leads us to doubt our passions, our interests, and sometimes even undermine our own skills. This incongruence leads to impostor syndrome, amplifies self-doubt, and minimizes self-trust. We feel like we need to be/do/act the way someone else does in order to be noticed, to be taken seriously, to fundraise. Our limiting inner beliefs don't match the limitless and powerful vision we have for our mission. As a result, our impact suffers and the mission never sees the light of day.

On one of my podcast episodes, I interviewed fundraiser Mimosa Kabir. We spoke about impostor syndrome and how it affects each of us differently.

Impostor syndrome, according to the *Harvard Business Review* is "loosely defined as **doubting your abilities and feeling like a fraud**. It disproportionately affects high-achieving people, who find it difficult to accept their accomplishments. Many question whether they're deserving of accolades."

Have you ever felt like this? Perhaps you feel like you're not qualified enough to be fundraising because you . . . (insert the emotions, thoughts, and beliefs that surface). Or maybe you're really good at connecting with people, but you feel like you need to be like someone else and adapt their "sales and pitching" skills.

The truth is, who you are **is** enough. In fact, it's better than enough. Who you are is fantastic, and I want you to share that amazingness with your donors. Are there skills you can refine? Yes. We all have room for growth and refinement. But does that make you a write-off or an impostor? No.

Impostor syndrome seems to be more prevalent for people who don't see themselves reflected in the leadership around them. I see this a lot with organizations who buy into the dichotomy of the "haves" versus the "have-nots" I talked about in Chapter 3. We think we have to put on a mask so that we can pass as comfortable and "fitting in" with the "haves" (our donors). I've also seen this with organizations that try to put only their "polished" staff in front of donors. Seriously. I have been asked not to include staff in donor meetings—staff who were amazing subject matter experts and deeply passionate—because they didn't present in a way that looked like the donors. Not only is this highly inappropriate, but it reinforces the belief that donors are separate from the work. They are not. If your donors can't handle the authentic you or your team, then maybe you should stop asking them for money and find new donors.

SYMPTOMS OF IMPOSTOR SYNDROME

- **Feeling as though you don't know anything.** In my interview with Mimosa Kabir, she challenges us by asking, "Does anyone even know everything?" And it's so true! There are things we don't even realize we don't know until we are faced with a particular moment or situation. We are all learning and continue to evolve every day. No one knows absolutely everything—we're in this together!
- **Feeling like you're not as qualified as others.** If Kanye West can run for President of the United States, you can apply for that job you insist you're not qualified for, or fundraise and connect with donors or supporters who are dying to give to your mission! Don't miss out on opportunities because you don't feel as though you're good enough. Channel your inner Kanye (okay, maybe not Kanye, but whatever public figure you admire) and just go for it! Your fundraising vision needs you to be intrepid!

- **"I can't do this."** It's easy to equate tasks that you don't like to tasks that you can't do. Again, that's your brain keeping you safe and in your comfort zone. Start small and you will realize you can do this, and you might actually like doing this.

Now, if this is the self-talk that takes place all day, every day, of course your mind will ingrain these beliefs. Repetition, consistency, and neural pathways, remember? Even if you did experience certain scenarios in the past, which then influences and impacts how you show up currently, it is possible to reframe and rewire your thought patterns and behavior.

Here are some ways you can do that.

- **Consider the worst possible scenario.** Ask yourself, "On a scale of 1–10, 10 being the worst-case scenario, how bad would it be if this happened? How would I deal with this?" We are primed to have a doomsday mentality when in reality, things aren't as bad as they might seem. What if that person doesn't return my email? What if they say no to a gift? What if—gasp—they unsubscribe from our newsletter?
- **Would you talk to your best friend or a stranger the way you talk to yourself?** If your answer is no, take a moment to really think about that. Treat yourself with the same kindness, empathy, and love that you would a friend or even a complete stranger. How we talk to ourselves is even more important. It takes conscious work to reprogram our self-talk, especially if all around us, we're surrounded by Negative Nancys and Pessimistic Petes (to anyone reading this who is named Nancy or Peter, I'm not talking about you!).

Let's upgrade those fundraising beliefs by taking a moment to reset. Sometimes, it's easy to get caught up with our heads down, focused on all the nitty-gritty that needs to be taken care of, and forget our *why*. In another podcast interview featuring one of my former students, Yvonne Harding, she shared the following tips with me how we can hit the mental reset button and anchor into our *why*.

- **Get inspired by your donors.** If you're feeling unmotivated, pick up the phone and call your donors to understand them as people and their reason for supporting your organization. That's often a great energy booster! Sometimes, you need to tap into the excitement and energy of your supporters who are die-hard raving fans of your mission so you can get your mojo back and remind yourself why you started this mission in the first place. Stay tuned because we're going to cover all things donor calls in the next section.

- **Prioritize what's important and allocate time for fundraising.** Instead of always playing catch-up, identify what's truly important (and sometimes those things might not seem urgent), and make sure you allocate time in your schedule to do the important things. Go back to the Eisenhower Matrix!

- **Go back to your vision.** At this point, you should already have a clear picture of what can be accomplished if I wrote you a really large check (the monetary amount, not a super-sized photo-op check). Go back to that. Revisit that version of yourself and your organization. Sit with the possibilities of what that money would do for your mission.

Part of being a fundraiser, being a social changemaker, a leader who moves like they mean it, is to think of yourself as one. You don't have to be/do/look a certain way to lead. You just need to be yourself and start with the smallest of actions that will get you closer to your fundraising goal. And if you're doubting your impact or thinking that you're not one of the big players in the sector or you don't have as many resources, just think of the impact a teeny mosquito has. Right?! For me, a single mosquito buzzing about my bedroom at night feels a little like a nightmare. It's tiny but mighty and definitely gets noticed. Of course, I'm not saying you should become an annoying pest, but it does make you see how size doesn't really matter when it comes to impact. Another analogy (maybe you don't mind mosquitos as much as I do) is the small but mighty mustard seed. A tiny seed grows into an impressive tree. From those seeds and leaves, we have mustard (my favorite condiment is spicy Dijon mustard), mustard oil, and in some cultures, a tasty dish (mustard leaves are cooked in a delicious stew with cottage cheese). Multiple purposes and multiple uses from one small seed that bloomed into a tree.

You already know that what may have gotten you here will not get you where you want to go, but that doesn't mean we just ignore what got you here. We assess it, we celebrate it, and we reflect on our next steps.

And assessing our fundraising past is a great way to upgrade our fund-raising beliefs, move through any form of impostor syndrome, and plant new, empowering beliefs. There are tons of great lessons and insights you can gain from exploring your fundraising past. It also helps to look at the past and fundraising history with a new lens. Now that you've done a bit of work drawing attention to those shortcuts in our brains, you might be able to notice when that negativity bias has shown up for you and look at the same information but in a new light (or new mindset).

Maybe there are opportunities you didn't see before. Or donors who you've been neglecting. So often, I see organizations always looking for new donors without caring for the ones who have already been giving. Plus, most small organizations say they don't know anyone who can give, but usually they are right under your nose. We are terrible judges of people's capacity. Every fundraiser I know has a story of the $50 donor who gave thousands of dollars or even left a major donation in their will. I've received a $25,000 estate gift from a donor who gave $100 a year to a small organization. I had a colleague get a complaint from a $250 donor and because she handled that complaint like a pro and really valued that donor's contribution, the donor turned around and gave $250,000. She had no idea what the donor's capacity was, she just acknowledged that a gift of any size is important.

So before you write yourself or your organization—or your supporters— off, take a minute to breathe. Double down on what has worked for you previously, while upgrading your energetic capacity and beliefs to match your fundraising vision.

Hot tip: It always pays to be courageous and full of conviction!

ⓢ DOLLAR FOR YOUR THOUGHTS

Get into a comfortable spot. This could be your comfy sofa, your bed, or even a yoga mat. I want to end off with a little visualization to help you raise your fundraising beliefs energetically.

Imagine your world when you believe that anyone can be a philanthropist, that philanthropy has nothing to do with the size of a check.

That philanthropy is an act. It's a commitment to support the change someone wants to see in the world. That you are surrounded by people who care about your mission and want to be part of the impact. That everyone who gives, be it $5 or $5 million, lights up when they give, because it's meaningful to them.

That everyone should have the opportunity to give back to the organizations that matter to them because everyone has a human right to make investments in the world that they want to create.

I want you to believe that you're here to build a legacy. You're here to create sustainability for your organization to feel amazing fundraising, but mostly to leave the world a better place than you found it.

I want you to believe that fundraising is a tool to unlock the potential of your organization. That fundraising has real, meaningful outcomes that can change your world. And the work that you do.

I want you to believe that fundraising is about inspiring people and bringing people together for a great cause. And for great impact.

How does this make you feel? Notice how you feel in your body. What are the sensations you feel? Write them down.

If you're feeling optimistic and ready—amazing! If you're still feeling cautious or skeptical, then I want you to dig even deeper. Why is your brain protecting you right now? What is the risk of believing in these things? Remember, your brain is going to be looking for evidence to disprove these possibilities, so try to suspend your disbelief.

If you feel stuck—because some of you might—now is the time to fully focus. Don't be afraid to look at what's still holding you back. Remember, awareness brings about clarity, which then helps you bring about change.

If you are feeling reluctant or hesitant or skeptical, I want you to write about it because it's important to acknowledge and address that. It's totally normal to feel a combination of excitement and optimism, but also still a little wary or hesitant. I want you to reflect on these next questions:

What's going well?

Where are you feeling stalled?

What can you do differently? Or what is the one thing you have been avoiding taking action on, but you know doing that one thing is exactly what will help you reach your goal? Schedule a time to get it done, today, and share about it on social media and tag me @thegoodpartnership and use the hashtag #reluctantfundraiser. I want to cheer you on!

REPLACE YOUR OLD FUNDRAISING WITH THIS

If you guessed that we are going to now get into some tangible action steps, you guessed right. Rewiring our neural pathways happens when we combine our new beliefs, thoughts, and actions together, and if you thought I was about to let you off the hook without taking a look at the actions that hold you back or let you out into the proverbial wild without a plan, you thought wrong.

Our actions reaffirm our mindset and either help us move closer to our fundraising goals or further away from them. What you do matters (actions). How you do what you do matters (habits). And who you are while you're doing what you're doing matters the most (mindset).

What I have noticed in my years of working with numerous fundraisers and smaller organizations is that people are far too focused on trying all the solutions and strategies they hear of. They have big, shiny fundraising strategy syndrome—always on to the next big thing, before ever taking a moment to assess their current systems, tools, and actions. You may have heard me say this before, but there is no one right answer in fundraising. I get asked all the time—will this work for us? What should we do? Is this the right strategy?

The truth is . . . I don't know.

What works for one organization might not be the right strategy for another. And we won't know what works unless we take a moment to assess our fundraising habits—what works and what doesn't work.

What does work 100 percent of the time, though? Something that is aligned and authentic. Something that doesn't just fund your mission, but actually fuels it. That reinforces, educates, and engages.

I'll never forget the first time I heard about a fundraiser called "touch a truck." At this event, there were a bunch of big work trucks that kids could climb on and into and explore up close. Get their photo taken in a tractor or cement mixer. Cool. Except this was a fundraiser put on by a small arts organization and the event had NOTHING to do with their mission. Sure, they raised some money, but those who attended didn't want to learn more about their work. They weren't interested in being on their email list for future art events. They were never to give again. And so, the organization spent every year trying to find all of these one-time donations from people who were not in it for the long haul (pun intended).

In this section, I'm going to walk you through some of the specifics about fundraising so that you can build those fundraising habits.

The best fundraising for your organization has nothing to do with what other organizations are doing. It has nothing to do with all the fundraising trends you might read about or learn about on webinars or in conferences. Authenticity is about finding the fundraising strategies that are going to resonate with your mission, your values, and your organization.

But more specifically, it's where those things overlap with your donors. That is where the magic starts to happen.

When you align your fundraising strategy with your mission and your donors, your fundraising activities become not just to raise money, but to really connect with people. And if you can do both of those, people are going to be with you for a much longer time.

CHAPTER 10

QUALITIES OF A GREAT FUNDRAISER

So often I hear people question if they are suited to be a fundraiser. I hear people think that being outgoing or extroverted makes them good at fundraising. The reality is that everyone will have their own approach to fundraising authentically, and that's great! We want people to feel like themselves when they are fundraising, because being a great fundraiser has nothing to do with personality traits.

What are the qualities of a great fundraiser?

Curiosity, consistency, patience, and persistence.

These qualities are the bedrock of your fundraising habits and the corner-stone of your personal and professional success.

Curiosity about everything—your donors, your colleagues, your behaviors and those of others, your patterns, your ability to assess what's working and what's not.

Consistency in your habits and in the long term. If you tried a fundraising strategy one year that didn't meet your expectations, it's possible that you just need to do it consistently to start to see results.

Patience to play the long game because fundraising is not an overnight mission. It's the impact of, and across, lifetimes.

Persistence to keep going in the face of rejection, doubt, and every other fear that will no doubt surface en route to your mission.

Let's start with **curiosity**. I believe this TRULY is the number one quality of an excellent fundraiser.

Donors give because they get something positive from it. You're trying to match donors who want to change the world with the organization that is creating that change. YOU want to find that spark or connection. Just imagine love. You want some chemistry. Right?

In order to find that chemistry, that spark or connection, you need to be curious, you need to **want** to know about your donors.

You want to understand what they are excited about, what their hopes, values, dreams, and aspirations are.

But it's not just your donors, you also need to want to know this from your staff, your volunteers, and the people around you. You have to want to know about the programs, clients, your work. What are their ups and downs, their successes, and challenges?

This way, you will attract the right donors, the right team members, and the right supporters who are all aligned with YOU and your mission.

Curiosity means asking really good questions and listening meaningfully.

Next up is **consistency.** This word gets a bad rap because we make it mean something personal about us, when really, it's action oriented and objective. Some of the best fundraisers I know are those who are doing these things all the time. I love the Steve Maraboli quote: "An inch of movement will bring you closer to your goals than a mile of intention." Small shifts on a daily basis will compound and create a big impact. Do the small things on a regular basis, no matter how mundane they are. The more we do things for ourselves and with our donors, the more they will pay off. I need not remind you that consistency breeds habits, which rewires your brain. This cannot be underestimated when it comes to your fundraising success.

I would rather have you do small informal things than try to do big fancy annual reports or donor reports. Plus, small informal things are often more authentic and aligned.

As much as we have advanced with technology, nothing beats connection. Good, old-school, heart-led connection. Pick up the phone or send a personal email. Better yet, if handwritten letters or notes are your thing, add that personal touch with a small card for your donors, staff, and anyone who is rallying with you for your mission. It feels personal, familial, and shows that you are tapped into the heartbeat of your mission on a daily basis. The more consistent you are with your fundraising efforts, the better your fundraising will be.

One of my favorite things to do with donors is to send them an email with a timely article about something we recently discussed. This doesn't even have to be related to the mission. It can be about pets (maybe we shared a love of dogs) or kids or hobbies. Showing that you remember that person goes a long way.

Third on my list is **patience**. And this is coming from someone who considers herself to be a very impatient person. But fundraising is really a game of patience. I want you to remember that while our donors might be excited to support our work, they're not necessarily always thinking about it.

For instance, we all get busy. It's the perfect reason why something will inevitably slide to the back burner, unintentionally. Sometimes, I'll have an email in my inbox and know that I need to get to that, and that is always my intention. However, I then missed the deadline because something else caught my attention.

I will never forget one night when I had every intention of supporting my friend's fundraising campaign with an online donation, but I just didn't get to my computer. My kids were having an epic meltdown; you know the kind where you feed them cereal for dinner just to calm down their "hanger" (hunger plus anger). I crashed so hard that night, and by the time I was on my computer again in the morning, the email had made its way down my inbox so it was no longer top of mind.

Life gets in the way. That's normal. Keep trying unless someone says, "No" or "Not right now, but maybe another time." This goes back to our mindset. We don't know what someone else is thinking, nor can we predict that. If we were mind readers, the optimist in me would like to think that nearly all of our global crises would resolve automatically. Thing is, we often project onto people our own beliefs. We make it mean something about us when we don't hear a "yes" quick enough from a potential donor or sponsor. We make it mean something about us when our requests get pushed aside, when in fact, perhaps, that person had a lot going on or maybe they genuinely forgot.

I'm going to step up to my soapbox for a minute (by the way, I tried to explain that phrase to my kids and they just didn't understand). One of my pet peeves is when I hear the term "donor fatigue." Your donors do not get fatigued. Maybe they aren't cared for well and get annoyed, but more often, this is just you projecting your own feelings and beliefs. Likely you just don't feel comfortable asking. Or you don't understand why someone would value giving to your organization so you worry that you're pushing the limits. Those limits exist in your mind(set). If you want to know how a donor feels, ask them.

My personal rule is to not put words into people's mouths or into their minds. Be persistent, follow up with them, but don't take it personally. I know you need money urgently, but cultivating meaningful donor relation-ships takes time. And you want donors who are with you for the long haul. Patience is of the utmost importance because the giving won't always come up front. Very rarely does someone donate the very first time you engage with them. In order for someone to give you a gift (that is meaningful to them), and especially if there is a significant investment involved, it takes time. It takes time to find that spark, time to nurture that spark. And the most meaningful part of any relationship—personal and professional—is the ability to get to know each other on a deeper level.

So the next time you find yourself wondering, *why is this taking so long* or *how come they haven't said yes yet,* think about *how* you can move those relationships forward. The better you know your donors, the better you can communicate with them in a way that moves those relationships forward.

And lastly, my personal favorite, is **persistence**. Keep going, especially when it feels like you want to throw in the towel. Just when you least expect it, and especially when you are super close to hitting that goal, it can feel tempting to give up. Likely, the mind drama in your head and from the people around you continues to reinforce the fact that you should just give up (albeit without any malice). *You've been at it this long and it hasn't quite worked out for you. What makes you think this time is different?* If you are able to rise above this type of chatter and keep your head in the game and focus on your *why*, you will come out a winner before you ever win the physical prize. Persistence is crucial for all fundraisers.

For example, I was trying to reach out to a potential donor, even though people in my position for years before had all tried to connect with him. And not once had he ever donated anything. He was an alum from the school I was working at and everyone before me tried to reach out to him, tried email, phone calls, and whatever else. Finally, in came me, with my persistent ways. I confidently reached out via LinkedIn. I had nothing to lose and everything to gain. I mean, what was the worst thing that could happen? That I'd likely receive no response like many others prior to me? Game on. I reached out and wrote, "Hey, I'm going to be where you live. Can we connect?" And he replied, "Okay." One word. That was a step in the right direction. We met up and talked and I learned what he was passionate about. In listening to him, I was able to match his passions to our cause and mission. Nobody had taken time before to be bold enough to just reach out a different way, but it worked. Turns out, he appreciated the personal interaction. Literally, every single staff member had spent years reaching out to him without any success. But that day, the one day we met face-to-face, started a chain of events that led to him giving a seven-figure donation within eight months. Amazing, right? The moral of this story is that just because someone doesn't reply right away does not mean they aren't interested. Sometimes, they might just love connecting in a different way. You have to get curious and find their sweet spot, or just seize the day like I did. And some other times, they genuinely might be uninterested. If so, move on. Don't project your own feelings and beliefs just because someone's not answering you right away.

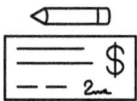

BONUS CHECK FOR YOUR FUNDRAISING SUCCESS

- **Stop playing the comparison game.** Comparison is great when you are using it as an expander, an inspiration. It completely zaps your life force (in pure *Star Wars* fashion) when you are constantly comparing your organization to others or your fundraising style to what you see professional fundraisers do. Focus on being who you are, with your natural strengths, and bring that to the table with pride. Ditch the big, shiny fundraising strategy syndrome and double down on what works for you and your organization and let go of the rest! Think about how much you can accomplish with the time and energy that you usually spend on playing the comparison game.

- **Play the long game with your four fundraising besties named curiosity, consistency, patience, and persistence.** Connect with your team, supporters, and donors in a way that feels good to you but works for them too. Don't be afraid to get personal. There is a human on the other end of that phone call or email or donation. Ditch the templates and the cookie-cutter ways, and curate your own unique blend of the above to drill down into your mission and get others onboard with it.

CHAPTER 11

EVERYONE IS A DONOR

Would you believe me if I told you everyone is a donor, can be a donor, and would love to donate?

Here's the thing: Fundraising is an art and a science at the same time. It's the marriage of creativity, connection, relationship building, and management mixed with strategy, storytelling, and tangible action steps (even the ones that feel mundane). It's this blend that, if you continue to master it, over time can only add to your success as a fundraiser and spread the impact your mission is meant to have.

Hot tip: Everyone can be a donor—they just don't know it yet. This is where YOU come in.

I remember working my very first job as a fundraiser fresh out of university. I was hired as a fundraiser at a women's shelter and was their first and only fundraiser. A couple of years into the job, we embarked on a capital campaign to raise money for a new shelter. And my board didn't know a lot about fundraising at the time. Naturally, we started to dream big, because why not? One of my board members had this *brilliant* idea that perhaps we should write a letter to Oprah asking for money for the new shelter.

My board members wholeheartedly believed that the ever-powerful Oprah would hop on her private jet and show up at our shelter, because again, these things do occasionally take place! They thought she would show up with the big check . . . the giant ones you see people hold on TV. That she would, in Oprah manner, grace us with her presence . . . *freedom from abuse for you . . . and you . . . and you too.*

Can you guess what happened?

We didn't even get a reply to our letter.

Surprised? Don't be! I see this happen all the time with organizations. So often, whenever I talk about fundraising, everyone almost always chooses to focus on the big donors. The ones whose names come to mind right away such as Drake, Ellen DeGeneres, Oprah, Gwyneth Paltrow, Warren Buffet, Reese Witherspoon, or insert any local well-known philanthropist.

These names come up over and over and over again. This is another mental shortcut that has been hardwired in our brain about what a philanthropist is. We picture celebrities (international and local), who we've heard of supporting a charity. We think it's anyone with some amount of clout behind their name and a flock of followers online. And we always imagine them having a lot of money. This is our mental shortcut that is definitely not working in our favor.

However, who's to say that Sally or Don from your gym won't be a donor? Or that the front desk concierge won't support your mission? Or perhaps the local mom and pop joint whose coffee and eats you and the whole office adore will be big supporters or donors.

But you already know this or else you wouldn't have picked up this book. It's time to expand your mindset even more. Giving is an act, not an amount. And by definition, philanthropy means the love of humanity. It's an act of contributing to a cause you're passionate about to change the world in the way that you want. Philanthropy is not about the size of your bank account. Or the brand of clothes you wear, or the car you drive, or the title behind your name, or the organization you work with.

Shift the way you perceive your donors, and you will attract more donors than you even know what to do with! And in fundraising, there's never a thing such as "too many donors" or "too small a donation."

Now, inevitably when I teach this, I always have one person raise their hand and say they don't have time to manage lots of donors who give small amounts and wouldn't it be better if they could just find one big donor? This is such a pervasive belief that I want to address it head on.

NO!

First of all—if you're reading this book, you've likely tried to find that "big" donor already without much luck.

Second—most large donors eventually end up coming from within the pool of donors you have already developed.

Third—it's much more sustainable for an organization to have a large number of small gifts than a small number of large ones. What happens when that one donor changes their giving priorities? Or when they get tired of feeling that your organization is too reliant on their funding alone?

I'm not advocating for you to adopt one specific fundraising strategy, but definitely stop making decisions because you think fundraising is "too much work." That's one of your mental shortcuts creeping up that you need to rewire.

PLAY THE MATCHMAKER

In the last chapter, I asked you to approach fundraising with the mindset of cultivating a new friendship relationship. That's because your fundamental role as a fundraiser is to play matchmaker between your potential donors and sponsors and your organization's mission and work. You want to find the people who want to change the world in the way in which your organization is changing the world.

You know the saying, there are plenty of fish in the sea . . . well, I'm about to take it one step further. There are plenty of donors in the world! If someone's not the right fit, you move on, without making it mean anything about yourself or your cause. Finding people, companies, and foundations who genuinely care about your work and are passionate about your mission is key. And those people exist everywhere, you just have to know where to look. Leave no stone unturned, as they say. Importantly, stop spending all your time looking in the wrong places. You don't have a lot of extra time, so start by focusing on people who care about your cause.

Recently, we were working with a client to run their first ever fundraising campaign. This is a small, local organization working with young people who have learning disabilities. Traditionally, they felt that their best potential donors were corporate sponsors. And while that was one good route for their fundraising, we decided to try to do a fundraising campaign where the youth involved in the organization would raise money (called a peer-to-peer campaign). This felt like a big leap because of the stories we tell ourselves about young people not giving as much or not having money. However, we were all BLOWN AWAY when their young committee members and program participants collectively raised almost $10,000 in less than a month!

Now, the moral of this story is not to go out and run a peer-to-peer campaign. It's that we found the people who were most passionate about the work and gave them a meaningful way to participate in giving.

As a fundraiser, your job is to connect with people who care about your cause and then show them how your organization is a great investment. The principle of "show, don't tell" comes to mind. Show them by the impact you and your organization have already made. Show them based off your passion and excitement about this mission. Show them how it can benefit them, what their contribution would mean, and what it would do.

My favorite analogy is if you are working as a fundraiser (or wearing your fundraising "hat") for an organization working to end climate change, your job is not to convince people climate change is a problem. That's likely part of your mission and organization's work, but when it comes to your role, when you are playing fundraising matchmaker, you need to find the people who already care that it's a problem and are ready to take action. Those are your people.

The same goes with foundations, corporations, or any type of donor.

Another rule I love to operate with is this: I am not here to convince anyone to join me on my mission. I am here to shine a light and attract the right people to my mission. If you ever find yourself overly persuasive and proving to someone *why* your organization matters or why the work you do is important or why the mission is important to them, they are not the right fit for you. If they don't notice your organization's value the first couple times, they're just not that into you. Time to save your energy and move on.

DON'T PROPOSE ON THE FIRST DATE

When you're dating and checking for compatibility, you take time to learn about each other's likes and dislikes. You actively listen and tune in for any red flags, and you most certainly lean into the moments that feel just right and allow that to guide you on your decision. But this doesn't mean that you propose on the first date, right?

Similarly, with fundraising, the most meaningful contributions do not come from a pitch or a proposal. They come from cultivating meaningful engagement and building relationships with your community, supporters, and donors. This is the type of engagement I discussed in the previous chapter—pick up the phone, send a personal email or a handwritten card, or video conference with them. Put in the effort. Nurture, nourish, and celebrate your community, staff, and supporters.

Love is mutual. Any relationship you have in your life is built on a foundation of mutual reciprocity that includes respect, kindness, and love. I want you to remember that because so often when we talk about philanthropy and giving to charities, there are often two polarities that occur. Either we think it is 100 percent altruistic or we assume people feel forced to give or fundraise. But people have a choice. We all have a choice. We show up when we truly want to show up. We give when we really want to. We make things happen in the ways that we can, when we desire to make them happen. To that same effect, if someone doesn't want to give, show up, support you, or make things happen, nothing you say or do will convince them otherwise.

From personal and professional experience, I've realized that people give because they actually get something from it—satisfaction, happiness, peace, a sense of community. It feels good to give, especially when it's a cause we care deeply about.

And everyone is a donor, can donate, and would love to support you as long as you are willing to show them the benefits they'd reap when they take a chance on you. Be it a friend or family member who wants to support you and your cause or be it a corporation, foundation, or individual, it is up to you as an organization to develop relationships with those donors and deepen their connection to the mission.

But first, repeat this to yourself every single hour: Everyone is a donor! Remember that as you focus on your happy matchmaking, fundraiser!

$ DOLLAR FOR YOUR THOUGHTS

It's time to bring out a few colorful sticky notes and make a list of potential donors and sponsors who would be on board with your mission. Consider this your matchmaking directory. There aren't any red roses to give out at the end of it, and some of your potential donors might not be the right fit, but this activity isn't about that. It's to help you expand your viewpoint and get really creative about *who* is a donor or supporter and *how* they can support you.

- Assign a category to each sticky note color: Friends/Family, Corporations, Foundations, Local Community, Individuals.
- List everyone you know.
- Take a step back and look at the names on your whiteboard or wall— how many of those people do you think would care about your cause? Take down those who you don't think care. Now, how many potential donors do you have up there? There is no right or wrong answer. The purpose of this exercise is to get you moving, get the energy flowing, and have you realize how many people there are in your life who will wholeheartedly support your mission.

CHAPTER 12

YOUR SECRET WEAPON—MEETING YOUR DONORS

Woo-hoo! Look at you fostering your fundraising mindset, assessing all your action steps, and learning to understand your donor. If you were to ask me the secret sauce to my fundraising success, it's this chapter. I mean, they're all important and crucial to your success, but this one in particular is the real-life test. Being able to meet with your donors and truly learn to understand them is the special ingredient to fundraising success. What makes them tick, what makes them happy, what are they passionate about. You're still a matchmaker, remember?

This is the one fundraising habit I want you to master and do on autopilot as frequently as possible.

Meeting your donors is an art. But one that I promise you're already really good at. No matter who you're meeting with—an individual donor, corporation, or foundation—this works with any type of donor because the principle is the same. Have the goal of understanding your donors and what they care about most. This is highly beneficial to you and your organization. It helps you communicate effectively, ask meaningfully, and successfully find more donors.

But before you go off on your date, here are some ground rules.

Let's start with what these meetings are—and what they are not.

Donor meetings . . .
ARE: An opportunity to get to know your donors and find out "what makes them tick."
NOT: Asking for money.
ARE: A great way to engage potential donors or get a buy-in for new opportunities.
NOT: Asking for money.
Get it? Good!

There's an old fundraising adage: Ask for money, get advice. Ask for advice, get money. The point being that everything is feedback. And you can do so much more with feedback and advice. It's crucial to your success as a fundraiser and as a small organization. Put it this way, would you like to receive an ask for money right away from someone who has just met you? No? Well, how would you like to be hit up for monetary donations all the time? No? You would feel undervalued, underappreciated, and the interaction would feel more transactional, rather than heart- and mission-driven. Now apply this same perspective to every one of your donor meetings.

The not so surprising part is that while you are *not* asking for money, and you are merely listening and sharing your mission from a genuine and sincere heart, you will likely end up receiving donations as a result of these meetings. Because your vibe is contagious. Even if it is information you are really after at this point.

For example, when I started as the Director of Development at a small healthcare organization, I reached out to every donor who gave just over $250 over the last couple of years and asked for a short meeting. I asked them for a coffee and I honestly said, "I'd just really like to get to know you. I'm new. And I'm learning about the organization. I want to learn about it from your perspective."

I met with one donor who gave $5,000 a year. Now, I didn't know when I booked the meeting, but in her mind, she had stopped giving to the organization. It hadn't yet been 12 months since the last gift, but she was unhappy with something and hence, to her, was no longer an active donor.

I probed further about what happened and she told me. I understood and apologized. I didn't minimize what happened. Nor did I set out to reason, justify, or make excuses. I witnessed her sharing her experience with me and I honored it.

I then went on to ask about her other experiences with the organization, which was a long-term care home where her father lived. She couldn't stop talking about how great the organization was. By the end of our coffee, she basically talked herself into giving again, writing me a check on the spot for DOUBLE what she gave before.

Imagine that!

But it's not just about doing one or two of these meetings. Nope. You want to meet as many people as you can. Have as many conversations as possible. Ask them to lay it all on you. Get curious about your donors and their experiences. The more you do this, the easier it is to fundraise. The more you do this, you will be able to easily identify similarities and areas of growth and refinement. And once you come to learn these similarities, your mind will automatically drum up more people who share these commonalities.

Some things to think about as you go on your donor meetings:

Where can you find more people who share these similarities?
Do they have similar hobbies?
Are they part of similar communities?

Think of this as crafting your wish list for your dream donor. What qualities do they all have? What about their hobbies, interests, and any other commonalities?

This information you gather by getting to know your donors is the foundation to having a good and aligned fundraising strategy for your organization. It's the starting point to creating effective fundraising and stewardship communications.

So, how do we book and conduct these meetings? I've got you covered. Take notes.

WHO DO YOU MEET WITH?

Take the path of least resistance and meet with donors you feel most comfortable with. This will boost your confidence and get you comfortable. It could be someone you know, or you might find it most comfortable with someone you don't know. Major donors, monthly donors, you name it. I've had organizations start with family members who were donors because that felt the least intimidating. As you continue to deepen your confidence, comfort level, and grow your fundraising mojo, you can then meet with everyone else.

IF you don't have any donors at all, start with your staff or volunteers. Start with people who have been close to your organization since you first founded it. Get their advice and feedback. Or maybe meet with people who are on your dream donor list . . . remember those colorful sticky notes with names of potential donors? Go back to that and look through them. This is a great way to find new donors or revive certain relationships.

And then book the meeting! I know it can be a bit daunting, but go and do the thing that scares you. I promise it'll feel less scary once actioned upon. When you are booking your meeting, be sure to let them know the purpose or reason for your meeting request. I'm a huge believer in letting someone know what to expect of your time together. Don't be afraid to be upfront and say that this is an information meeting only, that you want to get to know them, and that you're NOT asking for money.

Maybe you want to say thank you to a long-time donor, a monthly donor, or a major donor.

Whatever the truth is, say that. No need to fluff it up.

And then I always want you to follow through on what you say.

If you say you're not going to ask for money, don't ask for money.
If you say you're going to ask for advice, ask for advice.
If you say you want to get to know your donor, get to know your donor.

Why is this follow-through important? Because you are training your donors (think of it as rewiring their neural pathways) to expect you to always be upfront with them. It builds their trust in you. It positions you as someone who is sincere and true to their word. Also, if you ever do have an opportunity to ask in person (if it's the right strategy for you), you would tell them that's what the meeting is about so that they are prepared as well.

There is a full Donor Meeting Guide as part of the workbook accompanying this book, so if you haven't downloaded it yet, visit www.raiseitbook.com/bonus.

As much as I sound like a broken record saying this, here goes: Not everyone will say yes to a donor meeting. And that's okay.

Yes, you read that right. People decline donor meetings, and that is absolutely fine. It happens all the time! It doesn't mean anything negative about you. And you are not going to project your words or thoughts into people's minds and mouths, remember?

There have been many moments in my fundraising career where I've had people say things like, "Oh no, you don't need to bother with me. I'm going to give regardless." Or "I'm not important. I don't want you to waste your time."

And to that, I always reassure them. "It's never a waste of time for me to get to know you. We really appreciate your support, but I understand if you'd rather not."

The reason this happens is because once again, both fundraisers and donors have it subliminally ingrained that all fundraisers want is money. That asking for money is sleazy. It feels so uncomfortable because perhaps they have only had that set of experiences to compare to. However, you and I both know that you are different. How you and your organization do things is different. World class. Heart-centered. People first.

For them, I would clarify that you're not asking for money, but if they continue to indicate they are genuinely not interested in a meeting, don't push it. Move on politely and graciously.

Repeat after me: How many donors are in the sea? Plenty of them! And who can be a donor? Every single person!

HAVE A HUMAN CONVERSATION

I often notice many fundraisers go into presentation mode, when in fact, they should be having a basic human conversation. Connecting, engaging, listening. The good news is that you already have the skills to carry on a basic conversation. You can do this!

You are not presenting, nor are you interviewing. What this means is that you are not to lead with anything about your organization. Do not bring materials. While you may have some questions you want to ask, don't read them out in order. Weave them into a natural conversation.

Allow your conversation to flow organically. Listen actively—with your facial expressions, body language, and of course, mimic their vocal tone and language to show them how engaged you are. What this subliminally does is indicate to their mind, *wow, they really get me! They care about what matters to me. I'm not just some checkbook signature or cash cow.*

Everyone has basic conversational skills. What makes you an exceptional conversationalist is your ability to gently guide the conversation without really leading or controlling it. Listen to what your donor is sharing and engage actively with them based on what they're sharing. You don't need a script; you need to be human.

If they get excited about something, follow their lead. You'll get a better sense of what's important to them. Ask questions, go deeper. You can say things like "tell me more" to keep them talking and find common ground based on hobbies, family, travel, or anything else that might be of interest to them.

NEGATIVE FEEDBACK IS AN OPPORTUNITY FOR GROWTH

All feedback is great feedback—positive and negative. I truly do believe that. However, not everyone knows how to navigate negative feedback. And there is nothing wrong with this; we are human after all. And our nervous system gets activated whenever we receive anything that remotely makes it feel threatened or go on guard. Remember the mind loops we discussed in Section 1? Yes, your brain is associating negative feedback (that could very well be objective and all about a donor's experience) with a past experience that you may have had. This then makes you take things personally, when in fact, it's genuinely someone's personal experience either with your organization or perhaps something else they are dealing with. Remember, we are not mind readers.

Negative feedback is usually a sign that people care. And they care enough to be honest with you knowing fully well that negative feedback can be misconstrued or taken the wrong way. They care enough to put themselves in an awkward situation for the good of your cause. So when someone says something that might not feel so good, just say, "Thank you. I'm going to look into that. I appreciate your honesty." You can ask open-ended questions to get more information. Respect their experiences, witness their experiences, and honor them. Don't undermine them. Acknowledge and understand. Don't promise specific changes or resolutions if you can't commit. Most of the time, people just want to be heard. They want to be seen and felt. And whether or not they donate or support you, you can definitely make them have a more human experience. Show them you care.

DON'T LET QUESTIONS STUMP YOU

Often, most people shy away from donor meetings because they feel like they don't know enough or don't have enough information. It's okay to say, "I don't know, but I will find out and get back to you." There's much honor in admitting that rather than fumbling over facts that you're uncertain of. And this is a great opportunity to be resourceful and find out the answer so you can reconnect with your donor. It shows them you are curious, consistent, patient, and persistent. All qualities of an incredible fundraiser!

ALWAYS SAY THANK YOU!

We already know that people are incredible idea machines, yet very few of us execute them and put them into action. Everyone will tell you, "You should do (insert idea here)." When that happens, no need to refuse it or refute it. Just say thank you! Don't commit to doing anything brand new. And definitely don't say you've already tried it. Just be incredibly grateful someone cares enough to offer you some ideas.

 **Hot tip:** If you hear the same ideas come up over and over again, it's a sign from the universe that you need to pay attention to it and perhaps take action upon it after all.

When I was working at a university, I kept hearing the same thing from our alumni feedback that the school wasn't doing enough to engage them. When I shared that feedback with the Dean, they got defensive and explained that they were, in fact, already doing those things. But guess what, if you're doing something and your target audience doesn't know you're doing it, then there is room for improvement.

Donor meetings should be fun! They're giving you much needed insight on how you and your organization can make a bigger impact. From donor experience to client experience. Feedback in any way is a gift of the things you've mastered and learning what can be further refined. Once you've completed your donor meeting, send them a thank you card or note. I truly believe that when you give without any expectation, you receive much more than you can ever imagine. So what are you waiting for? Look over that list and set up some meetings. To take it one step further, share social proof with me, and tag me @thegoodpartnership and use the hashtag #reluctantfundraiser! I want to cheer you on as you head into these meetings!

(S) DOLLAR FOR YOUR THOUGHTS

You're going on that date . . . ahem . . . donor meeting. Get your best outfit on, a positive mindset and heart-set on, and bring curiosity with you into each meeting. Reach out to three donors today. Aim to have one meeting a week for the next couple of months to make this part of your fundraising habit.

CHAPTER 13

EVERYBODY HAS A STORY. WHAT'S YOURS?

Do you know what really connects someone to your mission? What is it that draws them to your organization and makes them want to support you, year after year? Your story. Not just how the organization started—but *why*. And not just the founder's story—the polished, professional version—but *your* story, your truth, and how it is interwoven with your organization—no matter what role you play—CEO, Executive Director, team member, board member, staff, or volunteer.

Everyone has a story, including you. Good storytelling evokes an emotional response—one that they won't quite be able to pinpoint just yet, but they feel connected to you and toward supporting you in some way. Storytelling is another integral part of being a successful fundraiser. You don't need to be the next best-selling author to be the best storyteller in the house. You just need to be YOU. It's true. You need to be authentic, raw, and master the power of vulnerability with elegance so you're able to maintain their interest in your story and be able to connect them to your story by sharing pivotal experiences.

By now, you probably know that I love digging deep into why we do the things we do and have woven it throughout this book. Buckle up, we're in for another neuroscience ride! Storytelling is a powerful way to build emotional connection with people, to help them understand the work that you're doing. But it also taps into some fascinating brain science. And being able to share a compelling story complete with facts, data, and real-life experiences? Priceless!

Whenever we hear a story, our brains light up. Seriously. It's as though our emotional responses are heightened as a result. How cool is that? The part of your brain that processes language lights up when it hears words, sounds, intonations (how high or low the pitch of your voice is, and any variations in tone and inflection), but when you hear a story, other parts of your brain light up that are activated by experiences. So it shouldn't be surprising by now that your brain can't actually tell the difference between being the subject of a story and hearing the story. Our brains put us into the stories we hear.

Remember the movie theater example? Whenever you are immersed in a story—on film or in a real-life conversation—your brain doesn't know the difference. It has the capability to be transported to that exact moment you're describing, even though physically, you're present in the current moment.

That's why, when you're watching an engaging movie, you get emotional because it feels real in your mind. You're transported to that exact moment in time, and your brain cannot differentiate between simulation and reality.

For this reason, we want to use stories to deeply connect with people's emotions and help them understand the work that we do and its impact. For instance, if you are part of an organization that provides a complex solution to solve problems (think tech, sustainable infrastructure, ecological solutions), storytelling is a highly effective way to help the community understand some of that complexity. Think of it as a way to bypass the logic part of the brain and directly connect with someone so they have a visceral understanding and appreciation. You can make complex issues relatable and emotional through stories.

Now I know what you're thinking, *why are emotions important when we have data to support our mission and its impact?*

Because we make fundraising decisions based on our emotions. Anything that requires an investment from us—time, energy, resources, money—is often chosen using emotions first. Emotions are the underlying driving force behind that decision. Our brain will use logic as a way to back up our emotional decisions. Recall the shortcuts our brains make around **Confirmation Bias**, or the tendency to search for, interpret, favor, and recall information in a way that confirms or supports one's prior beliefs or values.

Hot tip: If you ever want to change someone's beliefs, don't hammer away with data and information. That will just put them on the defensive. Use your story. And I don't mean to manipulate anyone, but to evoke, persuade, and ultimately help the person reinforce and anchor into a new belief. I used to work for a documentary film festival and it's amazing what a good story can do to change people's minds. We can change our beliefs through storytelling and emotions, and then the facts and figures and all the other details will then reinforce those beliefs.

Think about a time you purchased something or invested in something you deeply desired. You likely made a pros and cons list, talked it out with a few trusted friends, then voilà, you went ahead and made your decision. The decision to go for it or not stemmed from your emotions—on whether or not it would help you feel a certain way. If it would align with how you see yourself and your identity. We make decisions based on how we want to feel or in fact, to support how we believe we should feel.

Our fundraising vision is similar. We have a vision, yes, but deep within, we desire to feel a certain way once that vision is realized—be it giving back to the community or creating global ripples of impact. Whatever the driving force behind your mission, there is always emotion attached to it. *That* is what helps you anchor into your *why* and helps others buy into your vision in any way possible.

Imagine you're on a path to get a donation. Emotions act as the gatekeeper. We can't even begin unless the donor feels an emotional connection to your cause and mission. Then once we get through the gate, we can leverage different tools to help *reinforce* the donor's decision. Notice that I said reinforce.

The donor has likely already made a decision; they are merely looking for evidence to support that decision. The evidence you present (storytelling) can also impact the amount or frequency of support.

In fundraising education, we spend a lot of time teaching people how to write impact stories—you know, how a donor's contribution makes a difference. These stories are important, but your personal story—what gets you excited about the work—is equally important to fundraising.

Think of your story like a little matchbook you carry around with you. You use it to spark a flame in someone else to see if they care about the work. Imagine when you meet people or have an opportunity to speak about your organization's work, you pull out that imaginary matchbook that is your story and you strike a match. You tell your story. Sometimes, that little match lights a fire in the person you're talking to. They get excited, their eyes open a bit bigger, and they start asking more questions or engaging in a conversation. That is your first signal that this person cares about your work (and therefore might make a good donor). If they don't get lit up, then that's a clear sign that they are less interested. I use this technique instead of any elevator pitch, which is one of those bad hangovers from a belief that nonprofits should operate like for-profits. A good story trumps an elevator pitch every time!

Now, sometimes when I teach this, I have some people, maybe a board member or volunteer, say that they don't really know what their story is. Maybe they are volunteering to gain experience and don't have much of a connection to the cause. The best way to find your passion, your personal story, is to really get to know the organization and its work. Can you volunteer in a program and see the work in action? When I worked at a long-term care home as a fundraiser, I volunteered in their lunch program where we assisted with feeding individuals who could not feed themselves. Or when I worked at a university, I encouraged my staff to sit in on classes. If you don't have a story, your homework is to go out and find that emotional connection for you before you start to share that with others.

ⓢ DOLLAR FOR YOUR THOUGHTS

Grab your pen and workbook. We are going to dig deep and get into some storytelling, because trust me, you have a story that's worth telling!

1. What led you to begin working with the current organization that you're with? Why work in the nonprofit sector? Why this mission?
2. Do you have one aha moment where you felt like you knew you were doing good work?
3. What experiences in your life reinforce the need for this organization or mission?
4. What is one interaction with your organization that led you to get emotional?
5. Take it one step further and go live on social media with your story (even if you've done it before). You didn't think I was about to let you off the hook that easy, did you? We want to get you confident, bold, and fully connected to the heart of your story so your donors and community can feel that energy too! Tag us @thegoodpartnership and use the hashtag #reluctantfundraiser—I want to cheer you on!
6. Next, repurpose this live video into a social media post or an email newsletter. Reinforce your story and mission into the hearts of your supporters. Everyone loves to get a peek of who you really are behind the lens, behind the phone line. Go show 'em what you're made of.
7. Finally, keep this story in your back pocket (your matchbook) and just connect with people over it. Now, don't go into a pitch in all of your conversations. Weave it into conversation naturally. Don't start with the whole story; maybe start with a little hint or a conversation spark. If you feel deeply uncomfortable or awkward in having conversations,

I highly recommend reading the book *Captivate: The Science of Succeeding with People* by Vanessa Van Edwards.

CHAPTER 14

THE POWER OF STORYTELLING

You now know that the beauty of storytelling is that it has the power to move people into action, inspire and motivate them, and most of all, it lets them see a part of themselves in you, your story, and your shared goal. In the previous chapter, I shared some tools to help you understand your own story and how you can use it to find a spark of interest in others. Pull that trick out at your next cocktail party or backyard BBQ and see who gets excited.

But your individual story is not the only one you need for fundraising.

You know your work has an impact. You see that impact every day. You feel it in your bones. That's why you get up and go to work every morning. But do your supporters know and understand that impact? Does your team understand their impact? That if it weren't for them helping and rallying alongside you, this mission wouldn't come to fruition? What are their stories and reasons why fundraising matters to them?

Small organizations often struggle with how to communicate that impact. We live it and breathe it every day, yet we often find it hard to share it with others in a way that they understand and connect with the work. Sometimes, we get too complicated and caught up in jargon, and other times, we feel stuck in trying to communicate stories in a way that is authentic to our mission and work. After all, we don't want to be perpetuating stories that can be harmful to the communities we serve.

There are two more stories you need to have in your arsenal to use through your fundraising journey. They are: an impact story and your donor's story.

IMPACT STORIES

You already know that stories are the most effective way to inspire and move people. Instead of sharing statistics or vague information, stories are relatable and emotional. As such, they are the most powerful way to convey the work that we do. People can't relate to big ideas, but they can relate to one person. When we feel like a problem is too big, it feels like our individual actions don't have an impact. I know that every single donation to your organization has an impact, and you want your donors to feel that too. They need to know that they are part of a collective of supporters who are affecting change.

Often, organizations struggle with how to collect and tell stories appropriately. This leads to an all or nothing approach.

For some, they over emphasize the numbers, eventually pushing storytelling to one side because they consider it too "fluffy" and that "the data matters more" because "people care about the results."

For others, stories perpetuate some of the unhealthy power dynamics and structures that we explored in Chapter 3. We are glossing over complex issues to make them more palatable to our donors. We might be taking advantage of our clients to serve a donor's ego.

While we've already debunked that statistics are more important than stories, concerns about impact stories and not exploiting our clients are very real and need to be addressed. So, let's give you some tools to be able to tell stories in an authentic and empowering way that is aligned with your mission and respectful of your clients.

In my experience, there are two options when respectfully using impact stories. One option is what I call a hybrid story, which is creating a story that is true in a sense. We use these when we can't safely engage clients in storytelling. Maybe they aren't in a position to give meaningful consent. Maybe you work with teens or people experiencing trauma. When this is the case, we usually create stories that are true to the mission without it being about any one individual. Is the story true? Sure, it's not about an actual person, but for all other intents and purposes, it is truthful.

The other option is to use actual stories. Usually I do this with past clients or people who have been removed from accessing our services for a while.

I sit down with them and listen to their experiences in a pressure-free environment. We just chat and I take notes. I then go back and turn those notes into a story. The subject of the story then gets to read the draft and make any changes that they feel are necessary. They can opt to remove any information or details. They can even choose to withdraw consent to use the story if they feel so inclined. They are in control and have all final approvals. The story should feel accurate and authentic for them.

Another concern I hear from organizations is that they often see stories from nonprofits that over emphasize the negative or make the subject of the story seem helpless. This is actually another brain shortcut that's being activated. That might be how some organizations use stories, but certainly it's not how I've seen most small organizations use stories. Usually it's the big brands or ones that have big advertising budgets, and it's easier for our brain to recall those examples or pay more attention to examples that reaffirm our existing beliefs. So, if we believe that storytelling is exploitative, then we are going to see more stories that are, in fact, exploitative. Your organization's stories should be authentic to your clients and mission. And you need to tell those stories.

Storytelling can be a reclamation, a liberation, and a celebration when you help paint a vivid experience of who you serve and how you create change in a way that impacts their lives. In a podcast interview with Andrea Gunraj, she shared how sometimes a story or particular narrative can be overused. The aftermath is a desensitized audience, one that is miles away from your mission. It's important to recognize our bias, rethink our storytelling and engagement strategies, and ensure our organization is reflective of the communities we serve.

She talks about ridding ourselves of "poverty porn" and the "savior complex"—both of which are overplayed narratives within the nonprofit sector.

Avoid overemphasizing "poverty porn" when discussing various issues with equity-seeking populations. This means avoiding stereotyping in your language, your photographs, and visuals. So do everyone a favor and avoid the clichéd imagery of a homeless person lying on the streets. While this often does evoke a deep emotional response, it also dehumanizes the population you're actually trying to serve. It comes across as if you are their savior . . . or doing them a favor . . . meanwhile, that is not at all your intention or that of your organization. Your mission might be one where nobody goes hungry or homeless. Everyone is treated equally. Yet by showcasing and falling prey to this often-used narrative, it destabilizes the intent of your mission.

Along with poverty porn, the "savior complex" is also something that is NOT helpful in our sector. Whether or not we intend to do so, sometimes we position our donors as THE ONLY solution to our work, which is also false. Savior complexes are intricately woven with a person's identity— white savior complex, rich savior complex, and the male savior complex. Again, this is a problematic dichotomy of the haves (saviors) and the have-nots (our clients or work).

Do you work with equity-seeking populations? Is your organization on the front line of social justice change? So often we see our values challenged in traditional fundraising and communications and don't know how to reconcile our need to fundraise effectively with our beliefs and values. The good news is that we can still be powerful communicators and respect, honor, and empower the equity-seeking populations we work with. Challenge yourself to seek other storytelling methods and diverse perspectives. Maintain an open and objective mind and heart as you gather these stories.

DONOR STORIES

The donor story is one that often gets missed completely in fundraising. One of the reasons is that we make assumptions about our donors without taking the time to get to know them. You now have the tools to get to know your donors with your donor meetings, but I want you to take the information you get from those meetings and use it meaningfully for your fundraising.

The donor story allows you to understand who you are communicating with. Where does their story overlap with your organization's mission? That is the sweet spot.

I like to call the donor story a little twist on the hero's journey or your "customer avatar" as often used in business. Your donor is the hero in this story. It's important to understand this because this sheds light on *why* they care and give to your mission, and what they care about. Understanding your donor story informs a lot of your fundraising strategy and activities. The better you understand your donor's story, the more you see they are mission aligned and that you have a lot in common after all. And the more you know, the easier you can tell if someone is not the right donor for your organization.

In my free workbook that you received as a bonus for purchasing this book, there will be detailed story frameworks that will show you exactly

how to structure and share these three story archetypes. Please visit www.
raiseitbook.com/bonus to download your workbook.

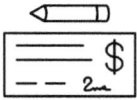

BONUS CHECK FOR YOUR FUNDRAISING SUCCESS

- **Authenticity wins every damn time!** Keep it real—in your tone, your
  language, your image. Make it personal because even though you are
  an organization or business, you're still a person dealing with other
  individuals. Nonprofit is human. People relate and invest in people,
  not bots.

- **Confidentiality matters.** There will be some instances where you
  cannot be wholly transparent about *who* the story is about. And this
  is okay. In our sector, and any sector for that matter, depending on
  who and what it is, you might, as a storyteller, be in a certain situation
  where there's an extreme amount of confidentiality or there's a security
  concern and you can't share that real person's photo and name. In
  that case, despite using a different name or photo, you can state that
  while the name and photo have been changed, the story remains true
  to that person's experience.

CHAPTER 15

THE GIFT THAT KEEPS ON GIVING— STEWARDSHIP

When we leap into the nonprofit sector—whether you are the founder, an ED, a volunteer, or a staff member—we are all responsible for managing, cultivating, and nurturing our mission, our donors and supporters, and of course, one another. Stewardship is one of those terms that we throw around in the fundraising profession like everyone knows what the heck we're talking about. But if you're a reluctant fundraiser, this might be a foreign term to you. Stewardship is nurturing the relationships with current donors and supporters *after* they give. At its heart, successful fundraising is stewardship.

Far too often, I see organizations put all their efforts into finding new donors, yet not enough time and effort is spent on nurturing the people they already have. This becomes a revolving door, constantly scrambling to find new donors only to have them give once and never again. This feels icky and transactional and reinforces most of your negative feelings about fundraising. Instead, imagine for a minute that the opposite was true, that your donors keep giving year after year. How much less work would your fundraising entail?

Another thing I hear from reluctant fundraisers is that managing relationships for a broad base of donors is too much work to maintain. Time comes up over and over again as a barrier to fundraising. If this is you, I'm going to give it to you straight. Go back and revisit your priorities. We have much more control over our time than we believe, if we can rewire our brains. How we use our time is greatly governed by the shortcuts in our brain. It's not that you don't have time, it's that your brain is deciding to use it on different things.

But stewardship is a fundraising nonnegotiable. It is 100 percent a must-do if you want to grow your fundraising. For every type of donor, stewardship is key to the longevity of their support. It doesn't have to be fancy or complicated. In fact, it's probably not a surprise that it needs to be authentic.

Just how it's cheaper to keep an existing customer than to find a new one, the SAME is true in fundraising. Not only is it cheaper to keep donors, but it's also more likely that you'll get one-time donors who become monthly donors or leave a donation in their will or even give you a major gift. The best source for deeper commitments comes from people who have given once (or more) already.

Your mission is of no use and cannot have the impact you desire and know it can have if you don't spend any time nurturing your community. Show up and get ready to connect with them. Stewardship is a habit. If you spend just 15–20 minutes a day doing stewardship, you will see incredible results and rewire your brain to love fundraising. Stewardship is your fundraising BFF where the cost of fundraising goes down, but your long-term donor engagement and revenue goes up. Organically. Hello, long-term predictable revenue. Cool, right?

LEAD WITH STEWARDSHIP

Being a steward of your organization, your gifts, and your resources is the most beneficial thing you can do for everyone involved. Oftentimes, people think it's more complicated than it is. Let's go back to being human and back to the basics of genuine connection.

Stewardship and leadership both have these things in common: transparency, communication, gratitude, recognition, and relationship building. Next, add in your best friends that we talked about in a previous chapter: consistency, curiosity, patience, and persistence. You've created a strategy that works for YOU, your donors, and your organization and its mission.

You're probably thinking, *Cindy, how do I continue to keep my donors engaged?* Easy peasy! Your donors continue to support you and your cause because they care. Because they also want to change the world, pave social change, and have global impact—all in a way that feels good to them. And giving to you helps them feel good. In your stewardship, it's important you reflect that back to them by showing them how they are doing good in the world. Show them how they are living out that narrative. Everyone loves to know how they have impacted your life or how they are impacting the world. Use that to share your appreciation for them, with them.

By connecting with donors in a personal, real, and raw manner, you build trust. This also means avoiding the use of industry jargon. They don't need to know that, nor do they care to know that. Write, speak, connect with them directly, from the heart. Be friendly, be you, and make it about the mission and impact.

If you've done your work to align your donors to your mission, you can also engage in hard conversations with your donors about the things that matter most. Stewardship doesn't just mean happy and easy. It can also mean facilitating important conversations or giving people the opportunity to speak up about what's most important to them. Stewardship should be authentic to your organization just like everything else we've covered.

CULTIVATING STEWARDSHIP HABITS

Stewardship, leadership, fundraising, and anything else you desire to master takes time, consistency, patience, and repetition. By now, you know the advantages of forming habits and their compound effects. Here are some ways you can cultivate stewardship habits so that you, your organization, your donors, and your mission can all thrive.

Our mind likes the easy way out of . . . well, pretty much everything. But you've already started rewiring your neural pathways, so yay! These practices shouldn't take up too much time, but they're really important to do in a timely fashion and on a regular basis.

1. **Thank your donors right away.** Basic etiquette, I know. But you'll be surprised to know just how many people forget to do this. Typically, if someone is donating to an online campaign, a thank you letter goes out automatically, right away. But that isn't the type of thank you I am referring to. What I'm talking about is making this more personal through personal outreach. Call me old-school or dated, but I love phone calls and I think they'll always be in style. I also LOVE using personalized video (check out my podcast episode with the team from Bonjoro, for examples). Some people might prefer a good in-person meetup, while others prefer a personal email or note.

   Hot tip: People will give more frequently and more likely higher amounts if they're thanked properly and promptly.

2. **Report back regularly.** Put it simply, people like to be kept in the loop. Many organizations spend a lot of time and money on their formal annual reports or fancy documents. However, you want to share updates on a weekly or monthly basis as well. Connect more frequently. This could be newsletters, emails, social media shout-outs, thank you events and gifts, and coffee dates (never underestimate the power of a good cup of coffee!). How you choose to report to your donors doesn't need to be fancy, but it does need to be intentional, real, meaningful to your donors, and something you can commit to.

Here's the thing, most organizations do not do these things that well. So, when you do them well (frequently and authentically), you're going to stand out. This is a great opportunity for small organizations to make a donor feel amazing for a gift that would otherwise get lost in the shuffle for a big organization.

SURPRISE AND DELIGHT! STAND OUT IN THEIR MINDS

Now that you've gotten the basic stewardship habits down to a science, you can steer away from structure and get a bit creative. This is the fun part. Donors aren't used to being thanked in a way that's creative, fun, and special. Either they get the form letter or email and annual report and that's it. Or commonly larger donors have come to expect familiar branded merchandise, food baskets, flowers, and tickets to a sporting event. So the more you are able to harness your creativity, the better. And again, don't overthink this. Creativity likes flexibility and intentionality. Creativity just means going out of the way to be thoughtful and put together something meaningful and allowing that to be your expression. Sometimes, it's the small acts that are the most meaningful. This is also a great opportunity to connect people more with your mission. What is something creative that means something to the work?

I worked at a women's shelter and a lot of donors were little old ladies who lived in the neighborhood. From time to time when I had a tax receipt to deliver, instead of mailing it to them, there I'd be, ringing their doorbell, with a smile on my face, ready to deliver their tax receipt because they lived so close to the shelter. And they'd always be surprised and delighted to see me. It made their day. They valued that human connection. It was a personal touch that continued to keep them supporting the shelter.

Stewardship doesn't have to be extravagant, but it needs to be mission relevant. It needs to make your donor feel special, seen, heard, felt, and appreciated. Allow your donors the opportunity to engage with your programs (it's not always the right approach for all organizations). It can be incredibly powerful. Put your donors on the front lines, allow them to see the power of their impact (donation). They will walk away with their own story of impact, and you will have really deepened their connection to the work.

I'll never forget when I was working for a documentary film festival, I wanted to invite donors to one of our school screenings, which is where we invited high school students to our cinema for a documentary film. The donors had never attended a school screening, but they supported them financially. Well, I filled the back row of that screening with donors, and the documentary was incredibly powerful. The questions the students asked were smart and thoughtful. Everyone was moved and most in tears after the impactful film. As I was walking the donors out of the cinema, one of them turned to me and declared that she was doubling her gift. Just like that. One simple, mission-centered, and authentic experience connected so deeply that it fundamentally changed how that donor felt about their giving. And it didn't cost us one penny.

Bonus! These experiences also help rewire your brain's shortcuts around fundraising, helping you go from reluctant to empowered!

$ DOLLAR FOR YOUR THOUGHTS

Grab a pen and your workbook. We are going to get creative and dream up some fun and thoughtful ways for you to help cultivate donor relationships that last beyond a lifetime.

1. What are some of the ways you have tried to keep your donors engaged? We want to assess what is working and what can be refined.

2. Create a donor vision board. The twist? This isn't about the type of donor you'd like to attract. This is all about brainstorming and visualizing all the fun ways you can connect with your donor, engage them, and get them involved in the front lines of your mission. This is about helping them engage with the impact so they continue to stay connected to it. Get artsy, creative, and intentional. Make this mission relevant. You can do this old-school style with paper or Bristol board. Or if you are more comfortable online, whip out Canva, an incredible app to create fun graphics for social media, and let loose.

SECTION 4

LEADING TO SERVE

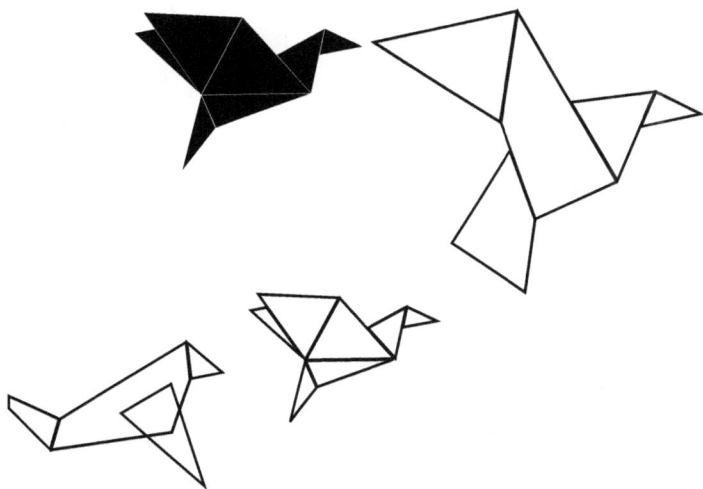

In his book *The Leader Who Had No Title*, Robin Sharma often talks about leadership as a call to servitude. To lead with a heart of service because when you come from a place of deep service to those around you, everyone benefits and everyone's lives change for the better.

When I first started this business, I had one word to keep me anchored in my mission with The Good Partnership: service. Why? Because when you lead to serve, you lead with a desire for excellence, evolution, and social change. You want to leave the world a better place than you found it. It's so simple, but it's so true. You listen and make decisions based on your mission and those you serve.

You chose to get into nonprofit work for a reason. This road, while paved with incredible intentions, isn't the easiest one to venture out on. Our sector is riddled with myths and narratives that keep us stuck in the status quo. That keep us with a scarcity mindset. That keep us from raising money for important work. But you're here because you know that the work is too important and it needs you and those around you, to not only be good at fundraising, but to feel good while fundraising.

You are a leader, no matter your role in your organization, whether you're the founder, ED, a board member, staff, or a volunteer. You are a leader *within* your role, for yourself, for those around you, and for the overarching mission. So step up and lead. But leading is not easy.

Yes, you will walk with fear, be confronted with rejection, and dance with celebration. Yes, you will be challenged to rise up, release old stories, rewire old beliefs, and truly repair the relationship you have with money and wealth. You will also own your greatness.

If not you, then who? And if not now, then when? This is the right time for you to position yourself as a steward of your mission, as someone who leads with vision, impact, and service.

When you lead to serve, you keep going, no matter what comes your way. This is called grit, and the people in our sector have it in abundance. You pursue impact over ego, and you show up with confidence, audacity, and pride for your mission.

You are nothing short of incredible! Too often we let our inner spark get extinguished with the day-to-day activities that are required of us, especially when we feel bogged down by work that is not aligned with our brain's shortcuts. When you can rewire your brain, it will jolt you back into your purpose, while helping you feel proud of your work . . . with an unapologetic confidence.

Most of all, serving does not equal selling your soul. Incredible things happen when mission-driven people confidently ask for their missions to be supported—monetarily or otherwise. You can do the hard things, and most of all, you can empower every single human being around you to be a leader who approaches fundraising and everything within it with curiosity, confidence, persistence, and patience.

CHAPTER 16

NOTE TO SELF—I'M NOT SELLING MY SOUL; I'M LEADING CHANGE

I get it. Although you got into nonprofit work because you deeply care about creating lifelong change, somewhere along the way, things got lost in translation. This work can be exhausting. It sometimes feels like we take one step forward and two steps back. There never feels like enough time, and there is always something more we can do.

Then layer fundraising on top of that. Fundraising is often seen as the "necessary evil" where we feel like we are selling our souls just to convince someone that our cause is "worthy."

You are not alone.

We have all heard the same stories growing up:

"All charities want is money."
"Selling is sleazy."
"Asking for money is bad."
"You can't be wealthy AND be a nonprofit leader."
"I feel guilty asking for money."

Perhaps you've even said these out loud to yourself:

"Fundraising is begging."
"Fundraising is the worst."
"It feels wrong to ask for a donation when there are so many other pressing issues going on in the world."
"If we ask for too much, does it look like we are greedy?"

The work you're doing to change all of this takes time, patience, and grace. There are times when you will be wading into the unknown, doing new things, and having your fundamental beliefs challenged. Change is uncomfortable for people. This is what we learned from neuroscience. Imagine an epic battle raging within your brain. The old ways of being (your autopilot) are trying to suppress any new feelings and beliefs. You might be making changes that are fundamentally better for you and your work, but your brain doesn't know that. It just knows that you are doing something that doesn't fit with your old way of being. The new feelings and beliefs are strained under the pressure of old habits. Being able to make meaningful change means to keep going. It's always the hardest right before your breakthrough. Forgive yourself for slipups and know that this process is not perfect. And you aren't perfect, which is perfectly okay. We all struggle with change. But change is possible, and now you know what's waiting for you on the other side.

Alongside rewiring our beliefs and mindset around money, it's important for us to feel grounded and safe on a psychosomatic level too. I often see people pull out all the stops and strategies to "fix" their mindset. But fixing your mindset isn't the only thing you need. You need to rewire *both* your mindset and your feelings around fundraising. When you feel safe on a visceral level, you will be able to *ask* and *receive* what you ask for. Have you ever been surrounded by all the opportunities possible (because there are tons, really), but every time you apply for a grant or put forth your ask with a donor or launch a campaign it fails at the last minute? Either the donor backs out, you barely missed receiving the grant, or your campaign falls short or doesn't launch the way you want it to. That is a mixture of your underlying feelings and beliefs, which we know manifests as self-sabotage. These could be feelings and beliefs around money such as learning to ask for it and learning to receive it. It could be feelings and beliefs around stepping into your leadership, owning your voice, and sharing your truth. Whatever it is, we need to help you create safety within your body so that you can rewire your neural pathways and anchor in these new habits and patterns you are consistently working hard to create.

Creating safety in and of ourselves doesn't have to feel hard or over the top. You don't need to jet off to Bali (*Eat, Pray, Love* style) or burn everything you've built to the ground. Anchoring in new beliefs and patterns requires you to ground yourself. You are rewiring a lifetime of old thoughts, patterns, and ways of being and doing that often weren't even your own.

These were ingrained through family members, friends, and anyone else you were surrounded with, as well as the experiences you had. But we now know better, so we will continue to do better.

Stop, drop, and ground yourself before calling that donor. Do a few stretches or yoga poses, or if that's not your thing, have a dance party and shake it off (Taylor Swift style), alone or with your team. Shake off that anxious, nervous energy and anchor in gratitude for your donor and how supportive they are of your organization and how connected they are to your mission.

Meditate or reflect, even for three minutes, before you head into that board meeting. Set your intentions and ground your energy so you can remain open and receptive to different suggestions and perspectives. Come from a place of abundance, not lack or scarcity or fear.

Remind yourself that you are supported, every single minute. You wouldn't be given this vision and mission without having the capability to fulfill it. So trust in yourself and in the universe that you will impact every person who is meant to have their life changed by you and your organization.

As you work to rewire your fundraising feelings and beliefs, I want you to remember that good fundraising—fundraising that doesn't involve "selling your soul"—means authenticity, mission alignment, and focusing on donors who care about the cause (instead of focusing on how much money they have).

Leading change is hard work. If you're reading this, you're probably already feeling burned out and exhausted. We all know the oxygen mask rule:

put yours on before you help others. This book is not meant to add more work to your already full plate. If you're feeling overwhelmed, go back to Chapter 5 and really evaluate what you are currently doing that you can let go of. What feelings and beliefs can you release? Letting go is hard and scary, but it also leads to growth.

$ DOLLAR FOR YOUR THOUGHTS

Get up and get moving. Breathe and get ready to shake it off. This is a bit different from the other exercises we've done so far.

1. Prep your space or work desk with anything that is a personal favorite that makes you feel abundant. This could be your favorite books, a mini bamboo plant (it symbolizes abundance), a fragrance that brings back a happy memory (our olfactory senses can recollect memories that feel good for us as well as the ones that don't). Abundance is a state of mind first.

2. Create a gratitude list. This could very well also be a future casting gratitude list where you give thanks for how many lives your organization has impacted, how many funds have been raised, perhaps even list all your dream donors who have said yes. The point of writing this list is to help you tap into a different brainwave altogether so that as you rewire your neural pathways, you are anchoring new feelings to ground and support that new habit.

3. What's your celebration practice like? Everyone has a ritual of sorts they do before and after they achieve a goal. What are some things you like to do before or after? Write them down. The next time you're working on a goal, big or small, reread your celebration practice. I promise it will make a difference to your mindset and your heart-set.

Hot tip: Celebration practices help you solidify the goal in your mind and act as an incentive for you to keep going, even when you want to give up.

CHAPTER 17

LEADERS EMPOWER OTHERS TO LEAD

Fundraising is not a solo sport. Now that you're committed to fundraising, you can't forget about those around you. Your success is directly tied to the rest of your team and organization.

I'll never forget my experience early on in my career when I went to my first fundraising conference and learned some amazing insights to improve our fundraising. A simple one was that mailed letters perform best when they are four pages in length and use personal stories. A simple insight that was researched and proven to work particularly well with our audience

of donors. When I presented our next fundraising letter to the fundraising committee for review, the number one feedback I received was that
it was too long and too focused on stories and not enough stats. In their
minds, fundraising letters were a nuisance. No one wants to hear from
our organization, so keep it short, sweet, and to the point. Of course, I
knew that our donors wanted to hear from us. They loved supporting the
organization and wanted to feel connected to the work. I was young and
less experienced at the time, so I changed the letter and let them rewrite it.

You will be faced with people who unknowingly are perpetuating the
harmful parts of fundraising or the stereotypes that just don't fit your
mission. So what do you do?

Maybe you can pass this book on and hope that those around you join
you on your journey, but chances are, they are struggling with the same
mindset challenges that also kept you stuck (until now). It's easy to pass
someone a book, but it's not so easy to get them to read it.

How can you bring others along for this ride?

LEAD BY EXAMPLE

Everyone wants to be part of a successful team. Very often when my team
and I work with clients, we find that the board of directors doesn't want
anything to do with fundraising. They want to outsource their entire mission, to put it mildly. But the whole fundraising industry keeps going on
and on about how important your board is for fundraising success. So
organizations spend so much time trying to convince their board instead
of just doing the work.

When we have a board that expresses they WILL NOT fundraise, we don't force them. We build a fundraising plan that aligns to where they are today, not relying on the board for help. We focus on raising money by taking the consistent actions I've shared with you in this book: meeting with donors, storytelling, and stewardship. And we raise more money. And we involve the board in thanking donors so they can hear how excited the donors are. We share the wins, big and small. We don't wait for them to act, but we involve them and show them that the organization CAN raise money in a way that fits their mission.

UNDERSTAND THEIR SHORTCUTS

We all want an easy, scalable answer, such as just do this one thing and we can get everyone feeling good about fundraising. But by now I hope you realize that this journey from reluctant fundraiser to fundraising superstar is a deeply personal one. It involves uprooting some of your deepest held beliefs. It's no wonder that there is no one-size-fits-all approach to getting everyone else on board with fundraising.

When you can, pay attention to signs to help you identify what their beliefs are.

Maybe all their fundraising ideas involve selling something. That's a pretty clear signal that they believe people don't want to give, that they want something in exchange because the joy of giving isn't enough. Your goal is to try to engage them in experiences where that belief is challenged, but in a gentle and loving way. Maybe you involve them in a donor meeting and ask questions about why that person gives, learning the benefits people have from giving that isn't transactional.

Maybe they gravitate to needing a fancy pitch deck before they are comfortable having conversations. This could be a sign that they feel the organization needs to present as large and polished because they think that's what donors are looking for. Or they believe that they don't know enough about the organization to effectively talk about it to others, so they want a document to lean on with all the answers.

Maybe they want to focus on corporate donations only. This could signal that they have bought into the dichotomy of the haves versus the have-nots.

You will need to start to decode their fundraising beliefs to offer solutions that help rewire them.

EQUIP THEM WITH A STORY

When in doubt, the most effective thing you can do to help others move forward with their fundraising is to help them find their own story. Remember the conversation spark in Chapter 13? Give people the tools to feel comfortable talking about the organization in a way that excites others.

Hot tip: There is nothing more validating than having someone else share your excitement. This alone can start to rewire those shortcuts and build fundraising success.

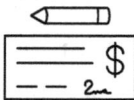

BONUS CHECK FOR YOUR FUNDRAISING SUCCESS

- **Empower your team.** Everyone loves to feel seen and heard, and for their impact and influence to be felt. Believe me, your team members (and your donors) are the lifeline of your organization while the mission is the heartbeat. No lifeline, no heartbeat, it's as simple as that. Empower your team to lead themselves, to be all in on your mission. Empower them to bring their ideas and perspectives to the table and execute them. Be the person who leads like the strong, swift, yet gentle undercurrent that makes the ocean tides rise and flow. You don't always have to be a hurricane or a thunderstorm. There is power in leading with grace, refinement, and deep self-trust in yourself and your team. Trust people to produce good quality work and they will. Become the best damn self-fulfilling prophecy for your organization.

- **Don't be the bottleneck in your mission and its impact.** While you can and will fundraise in a way that works for you and feels good for you, know that just because you can do it all doesn't mean you have to. Let go of control where you can. Release the desire (or need) to feel like you have to be in charge of every single thing that happens within your organization. That is harming your bottom line more than you can imagine. Refine the skills that you know you need to refine, such as fundraising, connecting with donors, and being at the front lines of your organization's mission. And release the rest that does not work or does not light you up.

CHAPTER 18

LEADERS DO HARD THINGS AND TAKE A STAND

Much of the mental shortcuts we make in this sector are much bigger than just our feelings and beliefs about fundraising. There are some big shifts needed for our organizations to achieve the impact that our communities need. The skills you developed about rewiring your brain can serve you in many different ways.

Think of some of the myths or harmful "truths" about your work and how you can start to change those too.

In a podcast episode with my friend Rickesh Lakhani, a passionate champion of grassroots organizations, we explored some of those myths that need to be rewired.

INVESTING IN OUR STAFF

This one has just got to be left behind. There are funders who won't pay for staff or overhead. If you don't know the famous Dan Pallotta TedTalk about charity, you should check it out. The scarcity mindset of our sector means that we feel money needs to go right to the programs and never to staffing or overhead. But your programs ARE your staff. Your organization IS your staff. They are your organization's lifeline, remember that. Investing in our staff and our team is key to the long-term sustainability of our organizations.

I've heard that many overwhelmed and exhausted EDs do not want to spend their time training staff because they are worried that the staff will just leave eventually and that it would all be a waste of time. So, the ED holds on to too much work and ends up burning themselves out. There's a now famous quote, where a CEO asks, "What if we invest in developing our people and they leave?" The worry is that it would have been a waste of time and resources. But the response could not be more relevant to our sector: "What if we don't and they stay?" What happens if we don't empower those around us to work better, to learn, to grow? What effect does that have on our mission and impact?

Our work is the most important work in the world, and we need to invest in those doing it.

WHO CAN GIVE?

By now I hope we've dispelled this one. We often make assumptions about who has the capacity to give and who doesn't. When we exclude people from giving just because we've deemed they can't afford it, we are taking away that decision from them, which seems pretty antithetical to our work.

We also often normalize the practice of 100 percent staff and board giving without thinking critically about it. Why are we expecting staff to give when we aren't giving back to them? If our teams are chronically underpaid and overworked, then it's probably not an appropriate strategy, which only feeds into the narrative that people have to be coerced into giving.

CAN CHARITIES DO HARM?

Just because charities set out to do good, it doesn't mean they can't do harm. Doing good and doing harm can coexist. In fact, many traditional or generalized fundraising practices can be very harmful, which is why we don't like them and fundraising feels yucky.

If we let people in the sector get off the hook just because they intend to do good, we are reinforcing racism, sexism, and other systemic issues. Make sure that your fundraising is aligned with your mission and is authentic to your cause.

SOMETIMES THE RIGHT THING TO SAY IS NO

This might be the hardest one of all. Maybe you've worked so hard to cultivate a potential donor and then they do or say something that shows they are fundamentally not aligned with your mission. Maybe your board chair gets you a meeting with the CEO of a big corporation that is part of the problem that you're trying to solve.

Fundamentally, money itself is not good or bad; we merely assign meaning to it. But can donors be bad? Well, they can absolutely be the wrong fit for your organization, and it's okay to say so. It's okay to walk away from money. Leave the scarcity mindset behind and make decisions based on what's right for your work. There are donors who are right for your organization, so focus on them.

$ DOLLAR FOR YOUR THOUGHTS

1. What do you stand for? What moves you as a leader? Write it down: "I'm (your name), and I stand for (list three or four of your rewired beliefs)." Repeat this to yourself every single day. Take it one step further and ask your team to do the same. Now, get emboldened and share it on social media #reluctantfundraiser and tag us @thegoodpartnership. I want to cheer you on! Imagine the wave you can create when your entire organization shares their personal mission statements.

2. Who do you have as a part of your organization? List every department.

3. Look through each department you've listed. Do you know everyone? Have you connected with everyone, at least once, genuinely? Do you know what type of feedback they have for the growth and refinement of your mission? Have you taken a moment to appreciate them?

4. Now, do the same for your donor list. You don't need to list every single donor, but mindfully, with intention, go through your list. Do you still align with your donors? Have you taken a moment to reconnect with them and appreciate them?

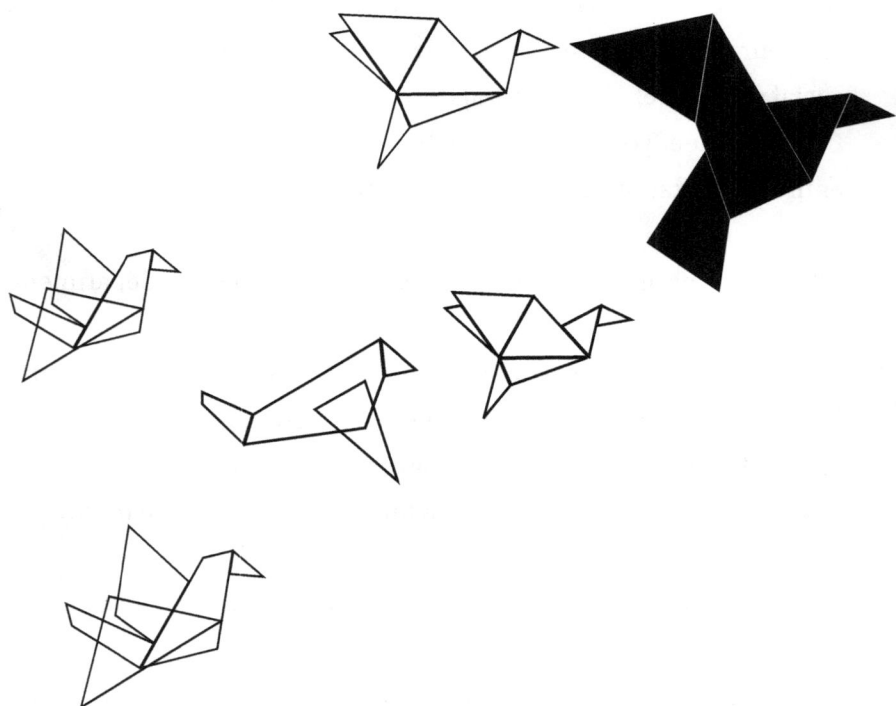

YOUR 70-DAY PLAN

I've said it before and I'll say it again: Whether you believe you can or you believe you can't—you're right. I know I wasn't the first to say this, but I do repeat it often. I frequently hear reluctant fundraisers list off all the excuses in the world why they can't be successful at fundraising:

- I don't know anyone who can give.
- I don't have time.
- No one has heard of our organization.
- We're too niche that no one cares about our work.
- Our work is too complex for people to understand.
- We need a stronger brand.
- We need a marketing campaign.
- We need a board who is better connected.

I hope by now you can recognize that these are narratives playing through your brain without your knowledge or permission.

Fundraising success comes from consistent implementation. The good news is that's the exact same thing that leads to rewiring your brain for fundraising success. You now have the awareness to know what's going on, and you are in much more control of your fundraising results than you ever thought imaginable. Keep moving forward. And when you stumble, get up and try again.

Remember that rewiring your brain takes at least 70 days of consistent action, so I have an action plan for you for the next 70 days. Let's keep it simple. Block in your calendar 30 minutes each day to work on fundraising. Here is what you are going to do with that time:

- Visualization and journaling: 5 minutes (see Chapter 8)
- Practice your story: 5 minutes (see Chapter 13)
- Book donor meetings: 10 minutes (see Chapter 12)
- Practice stewardship: 10 minutes (see Chapter 15)

It sounds so unbelievably simple. And it is, if it weren't for those pesky shortcuts in our brains. The work isn't hard. Anyone can do it. That's why it can be so frustrating when people don't.

Fundraising is a skill that everyone can learn. Much like walking or riding a bike. You just have to practice. And take imperfect action. Will everything you do be absolutely amazing the first time you do it? Most definitely not! But that's okay, because as I've said before, authenticity builds connection way more than perfection.

I'll never forget watching my son learn how to read. He was behind for his grade, so during the first lockdown of the pandemic, we enrolled him in a reading recovery program. Every weekday for six weeks, he spent two hours straight on zoom with his instructor learning how to decode words so that this seemingly random bunch of letters actually had meaning. Five days a week, two hours a day for six weeks. That is a LOT of time for a kid in grade 3. He went into the program reading at the level of someone in kindergarten and after six weeks, he was ahead of his grade level. That is the magic of consistency. Now, he plows through a novel every week or two.

I share this story with you because I know you can do it. I know that you are so committed to your mission that you can't NOT do it. You see the importance of fundraising to your ability to have an impact. And now you know that what you thought was fundraising was mostly in your head and that you CAN fundraise in a way that is authentic to you and your mission. There ARE donors out there who are the right fit for your work, and you don't need to sell your soul to do fundraise.

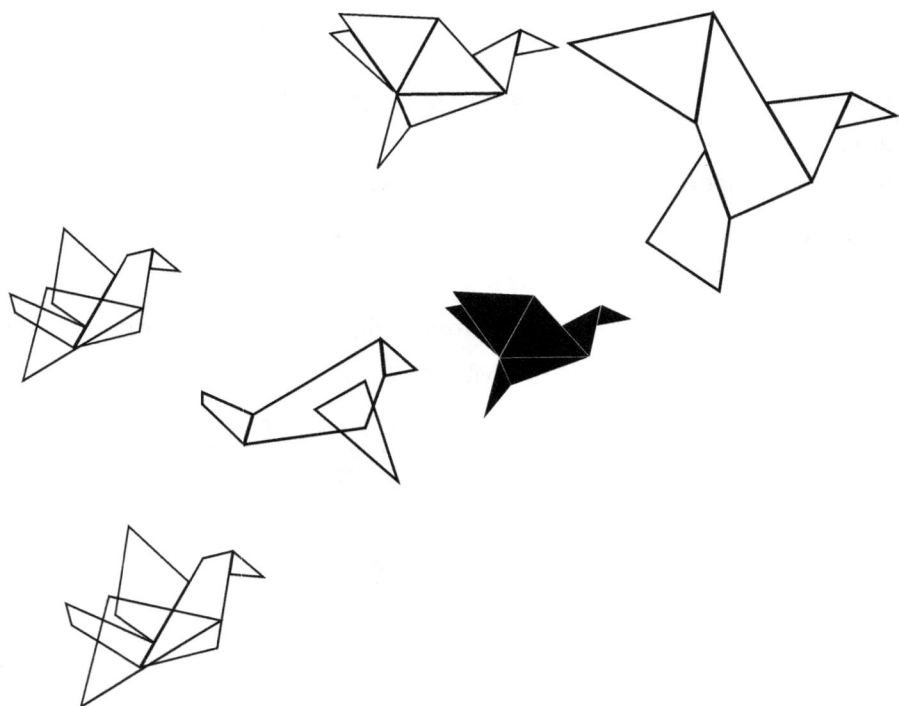

WHAT'S NEXT

I'm doing a little happy dance for you right now! You've finished the book and now have the tools to start raising money without selling your soul. If you want even more, I encourage you to check out these ways to continue your journey:

The small nonprofit podcast

Every week, I interview those involved in the sector and we bring practical and down to earth advice to, you guessed it, small nonprofits. Check it out at: www.thesmallnonprofit.com

1k in 30

Once you're ready to move forward with action, I've curated my four favorite ways for small nonprofits to raise money fast. These are the exact plans we've used with our clients, and I give you daily step-by-step instructions. Visit www.1kin30.com to get started.

Flipside Fundraising

If you enjoyed this book and want to find out even more about fundraising, we have a course for that! Flipside Fundraising goes even deeper into a lot of the areas we discussed with a community of support and more resources to help you implement your fundraising. Check it out at www.flipsidefundraising.com

Training and speaking

Now that you feel amazing about fundraising, it's time to get the rest of your organization or community onboard. Reach out to me if you're interested in training or having me as a speaker at cindy@thegoodpartnership.com and we can go from there.

RESOURCES

Referenced Books (with Inspirational Stories and Quotes)

Rising Strong by Brené Brown, 2015, Spiegel & Grau.

High Performance Habits: How Extraordinary People Become That Way by Brendon Burchard, 2017, Hay House.

"Cogito ergo sum": I think, therefore I am: the basic philosophy of René Descartes (1596–1650) by George W. Weiford, 1965, out of print.

Henry Ford: Auto Tycoon: Insight and Analysis into the Man Behind the American Auto Industry by J.R. MacGregor, 2019, CAC Publishing.

Unapologetically You: Reflections on Life and the Human Experience by Steve Maraboli, 2013, A Better Today.

Social Learning and Clinical Psychology by Julian B. Rotter, 1954, 2017 reprint, Martino Fine Books.

The Leader Who Had No Title by Robin Sharma, 2010, Free Press.

Captivate: The Science of Succeeding with People by Vanessa Van Edwards, 2017, Portfolio.

Goals: How to Get the Most of Your Life by Zig Ziglar, 2020, Sound Wisdom.

RECOMMENDED PODCASTS

https://www.ted.com/speakers/dan_pallotta

TedTalk with Dan Pallotta, "The way we think about charity is dead wrong."

https://www.thegoodpartnership.com/post/__036

The Good Partnership Podcast, "Engaging equity-seeking populations with Andrea Gunraj."

https://www.thegoodpartnership.com/post/___81

The Good Partnership Podcast, "Managing imposter syndrome with Mimosa Kabir."

https://www.thegoodpartnership.com/post/___84

The Good Partnership Podcast, "Overhauling your fundraising mindset with Yvonne Harding."

https://www.thegoodpartnership.com/post/__102

The Good Partnership Podcast, "Yikes—we said that, with Rickesh Lakhani."

https://www.thegoodpartnership.com/post/___112

The Good Partnership Podcast, "Collecting Courage, part 1 with Nneka Allen, Camila Vital Nunes Pereira, and Nicole Salmon."

RECOMMENDED REPORTS

The Giving Report, https://www.canadahelps.org/en/the-giving-report/;

https://www.imaginecanada.ca/en/research/30-years-of-giving

Harvard Business Review, https://hbr.org/

USEFUL SITES

https://www.bonjoro.com/
https://www.canva.com/
https://drshannonirvine.com/
https://www.ncbi.nlm.nih.gov/pmc/articles/PMC3747442/
https://www.thegoodpartnership.com/

ACKNOWLEDGMENTS

I want to thank some very important people in my life and career without whom I would not be where I am today, which is in a position to help others.

When I started consulting, I had a dream of building a company and culture that attracted the most amazing people and treated them well. I'm so grateful to the team at The Good Partnership, past and present, who also work tirelessly to help organizations do great things. A special thanks to Betty, Sarah, Kyra, Aine, Margo, and Eloisa.

Our clients. Thank you for trusting us with your visions. We love working with you and bringing you along our fundraising journey. Most of all, I love watching you celebrate your fundraising success!

When I started consulting, I felt very much like an outsider in the fundraising space. But I've been able to build incredible friendships with an amazing community of other consultants and collaborators. There are too many to name, but you know who you are. Thank you!

This book was no small feat, so I want to thank the incredible team who helped on the publishing side. Tania, Kelly, Doris, Christine, Michelle, and Sabrina—you are a dream team!

And finally, no acknowledgment is complete without my family. Chris, I knew you were "the one" when you came out to watch *The Vagina Monologues* eight times to support my work. Thank you for believing in me.

Lennox and Jasper, I love watching you engage in charity work at such young ages. You give me hope for the future.

Mom, Julio, Dad, Lee, Bob, and Alison, thank you for your love and support.

Finally, this book is dedicated to my late grandfather, Joss. You were so gifted at making every single person who knew you feel special and loved. I hope to carry that legacy with me.

YGTMedia Co. is a blended boutique publishing house for mission-driven humans. We help seasoned and emerging authors "birth their brain babies" through a supportive and collaborative approach. Specializing in narrative nonfiction and adult and children's empowerment books, we believe that words can change the world, and we intend to do so one book at a time.

🌐 www.ygtmedia.co/publishing
📷 @ygtmedia.co
f @ygtmedia.co

www.ingramcontent.com/pod-product-compliance
Lightning Source LLC
Chambersburg PA
CBHW071559210326
41597CB00019B/3317